God Bless
You + your children
& your grandchildren.

Michelle A Cir

Raising Courageous Children In A Cowardly Culture has been a Godsend to me! As a father of 3 children in their teens and tweens, I am always searching for parenting advice. The search is over as James and Michelle Capra address so many issues we parents face in our desire to equip our children to not just survive, but thrive when having to face the world of today!
Stephen F. Skinner, AfC, RPh.
Transformational Speaker & Health Coach
Author of amazon.com Best Seller in Christian
Personal Transformational Growth

"As Parents of 3, Grandparents of 12, and Great Grandparents of 1.... we have generation-ally been involved 'up front and personal' with the battle for the hearts and minds of children. Foremost, however, is the incredible impact that 'the home' has on the 'ever after' of children's lives. This book is a solid, Biblical, first hand honest report and admonition to raise Godly kids in this crazy world. Practical and applicable, I could not recommend it more, as a 'read' but more so as a 'guide' to daily living."
Naomi Rhode, CSP, CPAE Speaker Hall of Fame
Past President National Speakers Association
Past President Global Speakers Federation
Co-Founder SmartPractice, Life and Speech Coach

"'Raising Courageous Children in a Cowardly Culture' is a great book for young Christian families. I love James and Michelle Capra's hearts! Christ comes shining through. If you need encouragement, if you need to know how to raise children who are strong in the faith- this book is it! This family has stood the test of time. They have practical advice for parents and do a great job in explaining how each family makes a difference in our country and how raising children to be bold in their faith shapes our Nation!"
Linda Blechinger,
Mayor of The City of Auburn, Georgia

"Raising Courageous in a Cowardly Culture" is a must read for any couple who have or want to have children. Jimmy and Shelley have perfected a formula with a spiritual foundation that works, as proven by the successful lives of their six children. It is said "fruit doesn't fall far from the tree" and Jimmy and Shelley's Christ centered roots have enabled their six children to grow up into tremendous, happy and successful adults. Their personal stories and examples make this an enjoyable and content rich read that will bless any parent striving to be a better at raising their children.
Patrick O'Dooley
Speaker, Author, Consultant

Not a traditional "how too" child-rearing book, in Raising Courageous Children in a Cowardly Culture, James and Michelle Capra speak with forthrightness about the mistakes that they made as well as the successes they have had raising their children. I appreciate the intentionality they describe as they raised their six children. I believe intentionality, consistency, and communication are three of the most important things we need while raising kids and the Capras exemplify each in this book. Too many parents just let it happen, but not the Capras. They use their experience to encourage us all to "win the battle for the hearts and minds of our children."

Tim Madeira
General Manager
WRGN

As a parent, I sometimes questioned my ability to make a positive difference in the lives of my children; was I doing enough to prepare them to become morally healthy adults? Throughout this book, Jimmy and Shelly Capra share similar concerns and subsequently provide their experience in how they established a Biblical blueprint for raising courageous children who are called to thrive and survive in a cowardly culture and chaotic world.

John Bentley
Power2Transform

Raising Courageous Children In a Cowardly Culture by James and Michelle Capra is not only a book that parents need to have in their lives, but a book children and teens should read and understand as well. This book informs the reader about what it's like to raise kids in today's complex society and takes us on a journey that reveals the tips and techniques that James and Michelle employed while raising their own SIX children. Methods that are key to raising impeccable, content, one of a kind adolescents. As a reader in my teens, this book spoke to me, and although I do not yet have kids, I have benefited from the wisdom it imparts; how to deal with failure, how to trust in God, and how to recognize your own happiness. These are just a few of the things I gained by reading and learning from the experiences of the authors. James and Michelle not only the talk, but walk the walk. If you want to grow closer to your children, better understand one another, and instill exceptional values in them that will last their lifetime and beyond…read this book!

Cassandra Perkins
Radio host
Public speaker

Scripture tells us, as parents, that we are to train up a child in the way he should go. Jimmy and Michelle Capra's book is a terrific, practical and comprehensive guide for any parent looking for guidance in living out this command... especially in today's culture of tolerance.

Jim Lange

Founder of 5feet20.com and Author of Calming the Storm Within: How to Find Peace in This Chaotic World

"If we are honest, it is not the failings of our culture, a political party, nor the media industry that creates a lost generation. A generation cannot lose itself. It is the sole obligation of parents to ensure that instruction, wisdom and faith is deeply planted into the souls of their children. That alone will keep our kids from being loss. James and Michelle nails this truth! A sobering, practical and instructive guide for every parent."

Rick Whitted

Author, Speaker

With turmoil in our country and nine of my family members who have served in the military, this part of the book touched me so much that I want to share it on my television show and encourage people around the world to watch it on YouTube! ""Train the way we fight, fight the way we train" is a mantra I learned during my profession. An essential part of my training was learning that just because you are wounded, just because you are hurt, you must stay in the fight, you must do everything you can to fight through the pain mentally and aggressively and never give up. In numerous training scenarios I would here instructors over and over again remind students that getting wounded does not mean you will die; you must push through to fight and live." As a Board of Regents member and Director of Alumni, I plan to encourage each student to order this book for themselves as well as their family and friends! God Bless the Capras for this book!

Dr. Bonnie Libhart

Radio and Television Personality

Author of "Born Again Marriage" and "Putting It Together Again."

Jimmy and Shelly Capra outlines a blueprint to raising their family of six, in a way that has become controversial in today's society. With many households now operating without a clear path, and the politically correct system's attempt to influence how we raise our families, this book supports the age- old practice of allowing fathers to be the Spiritual head of their families. It defines the expectations of our children and uses God's Biblical principles as the cornerstone to a successful family life.

Charles Duncan Waterman
Author, Speaker, Realtor, "Journeys to Success- Give Birth to Your Joy"

"In a culture where traditional values are seemingly under constant attack, we need parents willing to step up and stand out from the crowd. That takes courage and equipping. With this book, the Capra's have provided both! As a parent of three children, my top priority is to pass on my values to them. This book is a tremendous encouragement and roadmap on how to do just that! Thank you!"

-Jeff Bloomfield
CEO, Braintrust, Speaker, Author

RAISING
COURAGEOUS
CHILDREN IN A
COWARDLY CULTURE

The Battle for the Hearts and Minds of our Children

JAMES L. CAPRA AND MICHELLE A. CAPRA

Scripture quotes from the New American Standard Bible
unless otherwise noted in End Notes.
Scripture quotations taken from the New American Standard Bible® (NASB),
Copyright © 1960, 1962, 1963, 1968, 1971, 1972, 1973,
1975, 1977, 1995 by The Lockman Foundation
Used by permission. www.Lockman.org

This book is a work of non-fiction. Unless otherwise noted, the author and the publisher
make no explicit guarantees as to the accuracy of the information contained in this book
and in some cases, names of people and places have been altered to protect their privacy.

ISBN: 978-1-4834-6618-7 (sc)
ISBN: 978-1-4834-6619-4 (hc)
ISBN: 978-1-4834-6617-0 (e)

Library of Congress Control Number: 2017902918

Because of the dynamic nature of the Internet, any web addresses or links contained in
this book may have changed since publication and may no longer be valid. The views
expressed in this work are solely those of the author and do not necessarily reflect the
views of the publisher, and the publisher hereby disclaims any responsibility for them.

Any people depicted in stock imagery provided by Thinkstock are models,
and such images are being used for illustrative purposes only.
Certain stock imagery © Thinkstock.

Lulu Publishing Services rev. date: 03/29/2017

Train up a child in the way he should go,
And even when he is old he will not depart from it!
—Proverbs 22:6

CONTENTS

FOREWORD

Some years ago, my youngest daughter, Genea, was selling our beauty products door-to-door in our hometown. A pit bull chased her in one neighborhood. When some of my friends heard about this, they asked why I would have my daughter out selling. They felt that as the owner of a successful beauty products manufacturing company, all I had to do was give my daughter some money. I told them I could give my daughter money, but I could not give her courage.

My wife and I fought to raise our three children, and by the grace of God, they are working successfully to make a difference in the world. My son, Joe Dudley Jr., is a MBA graduate of Northwestern University. He is a business consultant and is President and CEO of Dudley Direct. My oldest daughter, Ursula, is President and CEO of Dudley Beauty Corporation. Ursula is a graduate of Harvard Law School and was our corporate attorney before taking over as head of the company. My youngest daughter, Genea, is President and CEO of Dudley Manufacturing Corporation and owns a successful chain of Spas. Genea is a graduate of the Wharton School, University of Pennsylvania and MBA Duke University, and she serves as a board member of the SB Fuller and Joe L. Dudley Sr. Foundation. Without courage, our children would have been doomed from the start.

I share this information with you—not to brag—but as evidence of how my wife and I used Christian instruction to raise our children to be courageous. We taught them, set examples with our own behavior, and prayerfully kept God in the forefront of everything we did. We give God the glory for what they have become.

When we look at the news on TV, read the newspaper, or click on the Internet, we see glaring pictures of our children in despair. This concerns us because we seem to be losing the battle for the hearts and minds of our young people. Every day, our children are being attacked and destroyed by agents of the devil. The devil attacks their minds and hearts until they have no will to fight. He attacks them until they subscribe to cowardly thinking. By cowardly thinking, I mean they think all truth is relative and that right and wrong are not absolute. This is not what God's Word says.

In today's world, it is more important than ever to raise children who have the courage to stand up for what's right. In a culture that is more bent on accepting whatever is expedient versus what is right, we have to fight to save our children.

Do you ever worry about your children's future? Are your children following the path that you believe will lead them to success? Are your children associating with the wrong crowd? Do your children value and follow your guidance? Is your family growing stronger? What part does God play in your family?

If these are some of the questions you are dealing with on a daily basis, this book by James and Michelle Capra is very important. It examines and addresses many of these questions and may assist you as a parent. *Raising Courageous Children in a Cowardly Culture: The Battle for the Hearts and Minds of our Children* describes how they raised six courageous, Christian children.

The Capras' book is a must read for any parent who is concerned about raising courageous children who can succeed in today's world. This book is more than the story of how they raised their six successful children. It is a superb illustration of how success in life depends on having a "program" and the courage to make the "hard choices" to support this program. They followed the program God laid out in the Bible for raising their children. Read the book to see how they made choices and taught their children to make choices to support this program. Follow the program they describe, and I guarantee that you will have courageously successful children.

To get the same kind of results as the Capras, you have to choose to have a Christian family. You must choose to be a warrior for your children. You must choose to be a Christian example for your children. You must choose to have the courage to stand up for your children so they can learn how to stand up for themselves.

There is no greater glory than fighting for the lives of our children. God must have had faith in us to raise these children. Otherwise, He would not have given them to us. When we refuse to accept our role as warriors for our children, you see the results we get.

To get the best from this book, I recommend reading it with a notebook and pen handy. Write down the challenge or opportunity you are dealing with. As you read the book, God will give you the answer. Write that answer down, stop reading, and go do what God said to do. This is what I have done with great books like this for more than fifty years. Do this—and this book will change your life.

Get extra copies of this book and share them with your friends. We are in a battle for the very lives of our children. God expects us to act now. God bless!

Joe L. Dudley Sr.
President and CEO
Dudley Manufacturing Inc.
High Point, North Carolina
2016

ACKNOWLEDGMENTS

This is our third book in two years, and once again, this would not have been possible without the love and support of my coauthor, biggest advocate, and fan. Shelly and I have been together for more than three decades, and in that time, she has constantly loved me and sought to bring about the very best in the gifts that have been given to me. She has been—and always will be—my rock. She has made me better in everything I have attempted to accomplish, and she is the very definition of Proverbs 31!

I owe a great debt of gratitude to my good friends Phil R. Taylor and Kirk Massey. Throughout this project, Phil and Kirk continued to take time out of their personal and professional lives to encourage me daily as well as read, edit, and provide well-grounded wisdom, guidance, and encouragement. We are grateful that the Lord has placed such wise and godly men in our path.

We are extremely thankful to have been blessed to be the parents of six outstanding children who have continued to hold us up in their prayers and have loved us and forgiven us for our fallibility and shortcomings as parents. We sought their permission to write about their individual journeys, and they graciously and unselfishly agreed. We continue to witness and take great pride their individual pursuits in their callings in life with great purpose and passion.

Finally, we are thankful to serve our Lord, the God of second, third, and fourth chances. Throughout our walk and journey as a married couple and as struggling parents, He never forsook or left our side—even in our darkest and most frightening hours. We marvel at how blessed we have been in our walk and credit any success we have had to a God who simply loves and cares for His children.

INTRODUCTION

We are living in the most cowardly season in our nation's history. We are a nation of people who, for the most part, no longer pursue the truth in any arena. We have been led to believe—or bullied to believe—that there is no God and that the truth should not be spoken if it offends anyone. We have collectively decided that we have an unwritten constitutional right not to be offended by anyone or anything!

If some brave soul does proclaim to know and discuss the truth in an open forum, especially a truth regarding any moral issue, he or she is immediately accused of being a hater or a host of other derogatory labels that often result in the marginalization or silencing of that lone, brave voice. These types of assaults have created an immense amount of confusion and fear in the secular community and in the Christian community as well, which has had a stifling impact on how many parents are raising the next generation.

Instead of raising a generation of men and women of courage and purpose who have a common moral identity in the greatest nation on the face of the planet, we are willingly raising a generation of snowflake children who are offended by every spoken word outside of their close-minded belief systems. We are, for all intents and purposes, raising weak-minded cowards who have become drones in a politically correct society that continues to proselytize the false narrative that truth is relative and that one must believe that all views are equally valid to be tolerant. This twisted philosophy is suffocating the truth in our culture and forcing us into a type of immoral and unethical bondage.

It is amazing to consider that, in just a few hundred years, Americans have forgotten that our nation was founded by a people who escaped religious bondage and tyranny and fought for freedom and liberty, which gave rise to decades of prosperity, which has led to complacency and apathy, ultimately resulting in bondage again!

The assault on the truth is nothing new in our society—or since the creation of man. When Jesus stood shackled before Pilate accused of heresy and blasphemy by the religious rulers of that time, Pilate asked, "So you are a king?"

Jesus answered, "You say correctly that I am a king. For this I have been born, and for this I have come into the world, to testify to the truth. Everyone who is of the truth hears my voice."

Pilate said to Him, "What is truth?"[1]

That has been our mantra for decades and has led to embracing and accepting moral relativism, which is best described as nothing more than a philosophy that has turned into a pseudo-religion that asserts there is no global, absolute moral law that applies to all people, for all time, and in all places. Influential German philosopher Friedrich Nietzsche (1844–1900) is best known and studied for his writings on good and evil. He wrote, "You have your way, I have my way. As for the right way, it does not exist."[2]

In a culture that no longer believes and continues to do its best to kill off the belief in a merciful and just God, embracing moral relativism completely dismisses any notion of accountability and moral responsibility to family, society, or nation. If there truly is "no right way" that exists, I therefore am not and should not be responsible for the outcomes or consequences of my behavior or choices! That assertion is nothing more than a pile of rancid garbage. We know intrinsically that there is a right and wrong, and we can search for truth and know the truth. My wife, Shelly, the coauthor of this book, is the brains of the Capra household. She graduated college with honors while earning a math degree and a computer science degree. While discussing the question of what is right and wrong, she said, "If there is no real right or wrong, then one plus one can equal three. And if one plus one can equal three, how then are we able to build a stable house, bridge, or building?" There are absolutes and truths that we can't *not* know! In fact, one of my favorite Christian apologists is Dr. Frank Turek. He writes, "We often know right from wrong best by *our reactions*."[3]

As an example, I was talking to a very diverse group of young men and women at a leadership event held at Texas A&M University last year. As I stood in front of the group, I asked, "Is there a right and wrong?" Few gave a slight nod, but most nervously looked around to see if others would answer. I was taken back by the fact that they hesitated to answer the question, and there was a palpable reluctance to answer the question.

Finding no one willing to respond, I asked, "Is punching a newborn baby in the face okay to do?"

The entire audience erupted in shouting, "No, how terrible. Who would do that?"

We often know by *our reactions*. I went on to tell them that in all likelihood they would be taught and/or exposed by college academia and others that some cultures thought this behavior was perfectly acceptable. The young crowd responded in great disbelief with statements. They said, "That is ridiculous. That is stupid. That is wrong. Who could actually believe that behavior is acceptable?"

"Exactly," I stated. "So, is there a right and wrong?"

"Yes," they shouted together.

Of course there is right and wrong, and to say there is not is nothing more than a vile excuse to remain blameless and unaccountable for one's behavior or immoral positioning.

Why did this young group hesitate if there is a right and wrong? Because they have been taught what we call "stinkin' thinkin'." Their minds have been polluted to believe that one cannot express or define what moral, courageous behavior truly looks like. If no one is able to define this, then a society is in no position to determine morality.

The other reason for the lack of response is the fact that many young men and women have not been trained or prepared during their respective upbringings to face questions regarding moral reasoning. In fact, anytime I mention moral leadership, my audiences become a little nervous and uneasy. I find this behavior somewhat amusing because they have fell for the lie that morality is simply a personal thing. This is bull!

Morality, a noun, is defined as "conformity to the rules of right conduct." *Moral,* an adjective, is defined as "concerned with the principles or rules of right conduct or the distinction between right and wrong; ethical."[4]

Young men and women have been deluged with the exhortation that we can't push "our" morality on someone else. Who exactly determines the type of morality to follow? Better yet, each person must determine his or her own morality. Is that correct? Of course not, this is a recipe for disaster in any organization, in any family, and in a free society.

Our entire American legal system and the codification of our statutes are based on ethical principles and the moral law. Ah, but what is the *moral law?* According to Dr. Norman Geisler, the moral law is "the law not everyone obeys, but the law by, which everyone expects to be treated."[5]

Our democratic republic determined very early that individuals are expected to act and behave in a certain way for the safety, health, and welfare of our citizenry and country. While our nation is based upon the principle that all men and women are endowed with inalienable rights given to us by God the Creator, this does not mean that individuals can have it their way or do whatever they want in a free society. To suggest that they can and will is nothing more than the imposition of radical autonomy.

We are in a season that continues to worship at the altar of moral relativism in, which the fundamental tenet is that truth cannot be known. Radical autonomy left unchecked will lead to chaos, which ultimately leads to anarchy. Imagine applying the radical autonomy theory to any organization: individual employees deciding for themselves what organizational rules to follow, not adhering to the rules, behavior, or conduct expected by organizational leaders. The devastating consequences would be apparent: loss of focus, loss of vision, loss of direction, loss of control, and ultimately the death of the organization. The same can be said for a society, and the same is true for a family.

As Christians, we sometimes find it easy to blame academia for poisoning the minds of our children. Better yet, we blame Democrats, Republicans, atheists, or a host of others we believe are responsible. It has been our experience that, within the church community, we can be consumed with finding the villain, searching for the demon behind each tree that is responsible for our child's behavior. However, I submit, as professing Christian parents, that we need to be willing to look into the mirror and ask ourselves some questions: Where am I culpable? What has been my responsibility in training up and raising my children? Have I prepared them for the challenge ahead that is a secular world that openly detests and mocks our faith, purpose, and identity?

As a family, we have lived through seasons in our Christian walk. We have been exhorted to pull our children out of public schools and either homeschool them or place them in very expensive private Christian schools to shield them from the horrors of the secular world. Quite honestly, we never felt led by the Lord to do these things. And while this may offend some in our community, we have seen firsthand the dangers of attempting to keep children in a so-called religious bubble—never truly exposed to anything or anyone outside that bubble only to let them go off to college or to a fallen world unprepared mentally and spiritually for the battles that will come. Their lack of preparation makes them extremely susceptible to twisted philosophical lies and amoral musings, which can easily seduce them into the temporary pleasures that the world offers.

This book is about how we raised and prepared our children to face and battle a cowardly culture. We do not claim to be perfect parents or claim to have all the answers for how to raise successful children. This is in no way meant to be a how-to book. This book is about our journey, our struggle, and our joy as a husband and a wife over three decades and what it took for us to raise six outstanding, courageous children of faith and purpose who are called to live, serve, and thrive in a cowardly and corrupt culture. This book is also about hope. With confidence, parents can still make a difference in the lives of our children—no matter their age, our mistakes, or our current situations.

We do not have a set of magical steps to share that are easy to follow and produce great children. Throughout our walk, we have learned how children desire structure, borders, love, affection, direction, and security. There is no one-size-fits-all solution. There were times—rightly or wrongly—when we just shot from the hip, but we understood the importance of acting at that particular time. We have learned that we can do everything right in training up our kids, and they may still make personal decisions that impact their lives in negative ways. What we are saying, what we are crying out, is that we have a duty and a moral responsibility to consciously recognize that if we do not pour greatness into our children, if we fail to morally train them up, if we fail to give them a strong foundation of physical, psychological, and spiritual armor, they will be vulnerable to be snared by the trappings of a fallen culture.

My wife and I have daily raced into the arena to battle on behalf of our children and have done our best to prepare them for the fight that is rightly theirs to pursue. They each have endured challenges and adversity, yet they have grown to become light-bearers in a dark world, called to push back against the darkness that attempts to overtake our culture, our state, and our nation.

There have been numerous times we have failed miserably to be the examples we are called to be, but Shelly and I promised each other we would never give up our fight for our children, their spouses, and the children they will be blessed with someday. Our fight for them will not end until we are called home.

Finally, we humbly recognize that any success we have had as loving and caring, yet very fallible parents was only due to serving a merciful and loving God who has provided the ultimate example of what a parent will do for the children He loves.

James and Michelle Capra

CHAPTER 1

IN THE BEGINNING

I met my wife on the very first day I arrived at college. I was standing with a navy buddy who had made a pact to go to school with me when I saw Shelly running across the campus lawn. As a matter of fact, she ran across the campus lawn several times before we had the opportunity to meet. The campus chaplain introduced us a short time later—and he would ultimately marry us. When we met and talked, there was an immediate connection, and we started dating just two weeks later. Three months later, I asked her to marry me.

When we met, Shelly was a senior math and computer science major who was being recruited as a computer programmer by IBM. As I got to know her, I was taken aback by her confidence, her strength, her strong moral compass, and her firm beliefs about faith, family, children, and marriage. We actually talked about having kids very early on, and we were both surprised to find out that we both wanted to have six children. I know this will sound like a cliché, but I thought about her almost every moment of the day when we started dating, which could be why I didn't do so well my first few years of college!

After about a month of dating, I told my navy buddy that I was going to marry her. He thought I was crazy—and said it was just an infatuation—but I was certain that I was in love with this woman and wanted her to be my wife. Shelly had everything going for her. She would graduate with honors, be hired by IBM as a computer programmer, and earn a hefty salary with benefits. What I had to offer paled in comparison, but I had big dreams about where I wanted to go and what I was called to do. She became part of that dream.

I asked her to marry me on December 3, 1981. I got down on one knee in her dorm room with no ring—just a promise that I would love and care for her for the rest of my life. She said yes! We purposely did not tell anyone about the proposal over the holiday season. It was my hope that I would be able to buy a ring soon and then ask permission for her hand in marriage from her father and mother.

As the Christmas season commenced, I spent a little time at my parents' home. I talked a lot about Shelly and often bragged to my folks about her accomplishments. I was helping my father prepare an afternoon meal in the kitchen when he blurted out, "So what's up with you and that girl you are seeing?"

I paused for just a moment, but I continued to stir the pot of pasta. I said, "I love her, Pop."

He said, "What do you mean? You love her?"

I remember the moment like it was yesterday. I turned around, faced my father, and said, "Hey, Pop. Do you remember when I was a kid and I asked you how you knew Mom was the one?"

He looked at me and nodded slightly.

"Well, Pop. I know that I know that I know that she is the one— and I am going to marry her!"

Pop looked at me with a small, crooked smile, nodded, and went back to cooking. There was no further discussion. That was a good enough answer for him, and he never questioned me further. In fact, over the Christmas holiday, I had to ask him to cosign an eleven hundred-dollar loan so I could get Shelly's ring, which he did without question.

My father's family immigrated to the United States from Italy, and my mother's parents hailed from Portugal. My father was a Korean War vet who served in combat. Upon coming home, he married my mom, became a New York City police officer, and had seven children— six boys and one girl. My father and mother had certain expectations of their children: honesty, faith, and a strong work ethic.

Over the course of my childhood, thousands of times, Pop said,

"No matter what you become, be the very best at what you do. I don't care if you are a doctor or a garbage man, you be the best!" The "best" in my father's mind had nothing to do with moral superiority. It had to do with commitment, work ethic, and a man's accountability to his faith, his family, his profession, and his word. My father was very tough and ensured that his children developed a great work ethic and understood the importance of integrity, honor, character, and commitment. He had a tenth-grade education, but he instilled values in me that have been critical to my development as a father, as a husband, and in my professional calling.

I was a little nervous when I arrived at Shelly's parents' house to ask permission to marry her. Shelly's father is a World War II vet who served in the navy. His ship, the USS *Fuller*, an amphibious assault ship, received nine battle stars during his deployments, having survived multiple aerial attacks from enemy fighters throughout the Pacific. I was a young man with a big dream, asking to marry their youngest daughter. I had reason to be a little concerned, but they were both so gracious and supportive, and they welcomed me into their family as their own son.

Before we knew it we were married. Just two years later—after graduating college and being commissioned as a military intelligence officer—we were off to my officer basic course in Fort Huachuca, Arizona. We were very excited about becoming parents and really looked forward to having children. I had decided early on that being a father would be an easy task for me. I grew up with five brothers and a sister, so I was sure I knew all there was to parenting.

It would take me a little while to understand that you don't just become a fighter because you grow up watching the fights. The same is true with parenting. Early on, I pictured my children as perfect little soldiers—even better than the von Trapp family from *The Sound of Music*. Yes, it was a short-lived, glorious little fairy tale in my head. I would soon learn that my children were all wired a little differently with their personalities and talents.

In October, as my company arrived at Fort Huachuca after a week in the field on an exercise, my company commander approached me, grabbed my weapon, and said, "You need to get over to your wife right away."

Shelly, nine months pregnant with our first child, was waiting outside the armory. As I approached her, she smiled and told me she thought she was in labor. We rushed to the on-base hospital and were met on the OB ward by a couple of nurses who examined her right away.

Following the examination, the charge nurse told us to go home and walk around the house because she was not ready to deliver yet. We would wind up going back to the hospital two more times that day, and on the last visit, she was admitted.

Following nearly twenty hours of labor, a young army physician advised us that it would be necessary for Shelly to have a cesarean section. As she was wheeled into the operating room at about 3:00 a.m., I was told to wait outside until she was prepped. I woke up about an hour later to the pediatrician congratulating me on the birth of our baby girl.

Wiping sleep from my eyes, I asked the doctor if he was sure because for some reason, I was convinced that we were having a boy. The doctor just smiled as he wheeled our firstborn, Jessica Marie, to the newborn nursery. As I went in to the OR to see Shelly, she was already starting to go to sleep. The surgeons were closing up the incision, but she was awake enough to say we had a girl—and she was healthy.

In the nursery, I held Jessica and counted her fingers and toes over and over again, I checked the size of her ears, her eyes, and her nose, trying to ensure there were no defects, bumps, or blemishes and making sure everything was attached. After a mandatory five days in the hospital, Shelly and Jessica came home.

(As a side note, all six of our children were born via C-section. By the time our number six was born, Shelly would go in for the C-section and leave the next day. There was no more mandatory five-day stay. Get in, and if all is well, get out!)

We arrived at our duplex on the base to find that the soldiers in my company had filled the porch with enough diapers, baby wipes, and miscellaneous newborn items to last for six months! As Shelly placed Jess in her crib, our dog, a Doberman pinscher was extremely curious about the new package that had arrived. I decided to take Jessica out of her crib, and while wrapped tightly in her blankets, I placed her on the carpet for the dog to look at. Following a number of sniffs and a lick on the face, the dog placed herself at the foot of the crib, and she would remain there every night while we were stationed in Fort Huachuca. To our amazement, when Jess would fuss in her crib, the Doberman would run back and forth from her nursery to where we were located until one of us picked her up. It was if the dog was letting us know that the thing in the bed needed attention!

Although we were new parents, Shelly and I were very comfortable with our firstborn, not particularly treating her like a piece of fine china. We did jump up at any sound or cry, making sure she wasn't in any distress. From time to time, we received unsolicited advice from others outside our families who would attempt to school us on child-rearing, in particular when it came to how parents should deal with a crying baby. We heard a number of well-intentioned people tell us to just let the baby cry itself to sleep at night. We never understood—nor do we now understand—why we would ever let our baby just cry at night. She was a baby—not a toddler or a child! That never made sense to us. We both believed that when a baby cries, it is crying for a reason: the baby is hungry, the baby is uncomfortable, the baby is in pain, or the baby wants to be held. We were good with those reasons for walking in and picking her up. There were countless nights where our bed became the crib for the night, and we were and still are both okay with that.

There was still so much to learn about that little person we brought home. Is she eating enough? Does she sleep too much? Is she growing enough? Can she see yet? The list goes on and on. On one particular morning, Jessica was sitting in her swing. Shelly confided in me that she was worried that Jess couldn't hear. I told Shelly that I was sure it was nothing, but she was definitely concerned that something might be wrong. So, being a dutiful husband and wanting to alleviate the concerns of my wife, I decided to position myself in the front of the six-week-old baby girl who was sound asleep in her swing. I screamed as loud as I could. All at once, little Jessica's arms and legs flung out wide, and she let out a scream of her own. My wife quickly unbuckled the traumatized little baby from the swing. I exclaimed, "See? It's all good. She hears fine!" It was not very scientific, but Shelly—although somewhat aggravated at my method—was now convinced that Jessica did not have a hearing problem. At least that's what she told me when she finally decided to talk to me after putting our agitated little girl to sleep.

My tour at Fort Huachuca was fast coming to a close. It was late January, and Jessica was just about three months old. Shelly and I had hoped and prayed that I would be hired by the Drug Enforcement Administration (DEA). My application had been in process for about seven months. It was difficult to hear that there would be no more DEA classes hired until the following year. We were on our way back to New York and needed to make some decisions about how we would move forward with a new baby in tow.

We spent a few weeks between both of our parents' homes, getting reacquainted with family and introducing the new Capra baby to grandparents, aunts, and uncles. When we first moved to Fort Huachuca, Shelly requested and was approved for a leave of absence from IBM. Throughout our army tour, she stayed in contact with her employer—and they often asked when she was coming back to work. Within a few weeks of being back in New York, and after much discussion and prayer, we decided that it was necessary for Shelly to go back to work at IBM in order to meet our financial obligations while I was waiting to be hired by DEA. Within a few months of her being back at IBM, we settled into an upstairs apartment in downtown Poughkeepsie, New York where I began my brief stint as a stay-at-home dad while Shelly worked full-time.

As the weeks turned into months, it bothered me at times to see my wife go off to work while I stayed at home or tried my hand in starting a business while waiting to be called by the DEA. Although Shelly had an outstanding career with a great salary and benefits and the potential to move up quickly in her organization, we both longed for and prayed that the Lord would answer my prayer to be called to public service. You see, it is important for the reader to understand that what attracted us to each other was that we were equally yoked in faith, in purpose, and in our beliefs in how we would raise a family. I believed and desired to be the provider as well as the spiritual head of our family, while Shelly believed and desired to be home full-time as a mother, a wife, and the heart of our family. We would talk for hours on this matter long before we were married and had prayed that we would be able to fulfill these roles as a husband and wife and as parents. We never gave a rat's bottom about what other people thought about our motives and decisions to live our life and raise our family. We have never really cared if other so-called progressive young or older parents thought that our decisions to walk our faith and our life were somehow sexist, draconian, or close-minded. What really mattered to us was that we sought advice and counsel from each other and from the God we serve.

The call that we had been waiting for finally came on Christmas Eve 1986. I was offered a job as a special agent with the Drug Enforcement Administration. By February 1987, we had moved out of our apartment, put most of our belongings in storage, and moved Shelly and Jessica, now just about sixteen months old, to my parents' house in upstate New York. We were very blessed that my parents, who raised seven of their own children and were empty nesters, were more than willing to watch and care for Jessica while I was at the DEA Academy and while Shelly made the 100-mile round-trip to work every day.

After three months, I was finally authorized to go home for the weekend to visit with Shelly and Jessica. I could already see that Jessica was becoming very independent, very sure of herself, and not afraid of anything. She was developing an air of confidence about her even at her very tender young age. I remember looking at her and thinking she was born and designed to be the oldest child in our family.

Following graduation from the DEA Academy, I spent three months working in the streets of Manhattan before transferring to Los Angeles. We had already moved so many times since we were married that Shelly's dad referred to us as "Lewis and Clark." Once again, Shelly took a leave of absence that would ultimately be permanent. We gathered our belongings, packed up the car, and headed out to our new journey and life in California. We were very excited about the move, excited about my career, and excited about the great news that we had another child on the way. During our time in Los Angeles, we would see our family blessed and growing while dealing with the challenges and joys of parenthood.

CHAPTER 2

DEVELOPING AN ARMOR
OF CONFIDENCE

We were stationed in Los Angeles from August 1987 until July 1996. During that time, Shelly gave birth to the remaining five of six Capra children: Douglas, Mark, Rebecca, Marissa, and Micah.

A few years after arriving, we moved into our first home in San Dimas, California, just thirty-five miles east of downtown Los Angeles. By the time we left, we were a family of eight, including a dog, two parakeets, and a cat all living in a 1,050-square-foot home! It never dawned on us that the house was small for such a big family because we loved our little home at the end of the cul-de-sac. Shelly was—and still is—an amazing housekeeper and kept the house impeccably clean. We would often get questioned by friends how this was possible. As a matter of fact, the kids still tease Shelly and say that she is not happy if she isn't using bleach and a mop on something!

It soon became apparent that as the children arrived, although they shared many similar traits, they were each wired a little differently. Their personalities and their gifts began to manifest very early in their lives. From the moment the children were born, Shelly and I always believed that raising them was our responsibility—not schools, teachers, churches, or civic organizations. Certainly those institutions are good, but we would not divest our responsibility or our authority to them.

I often couched our responsibility as warriors who enter the arena in order to fight for the hearts and minds of our children. We believe that a parent who defines his or her role as a true warrior is a man or woman of purpose and integrity; one who is engaged aggressively or energetically in a battle, cause, or conflict. How many readers can describe raising children, being married or sometimes just living life like being in a battle, conflict, or cause? The arena for us was the ability to daily make time to pour lessons and greatness into each of our children. Our focus on this training was to intentionally help the children develop an armor of confidence as they went off to school, which would prepare them to deal with the social, physical, and intellectual challenges ahead.

Our battle strategy started early in their lives, jumping into the arena and talking to our kids at a very early age about everything! There was no topic that couldn't be fought in the arena! We learned early on that being in the arena prepared us to lead, love, train, discipline, and be the example of excellence—not perfection. In my law enforcement profession, there is a tactical truth that states, "Train the way you fight, and you will fight the way you train." It is really akin to "reaping what you sow." We believed it was more than our job as parents; it was our moral responsibility to train up our children and prepare them to face the battles that would be ahead of them.

During our time in California, we began to instill habits and routines with the kids as they grew. First and foremost was taking time to pray at night before they went to sleep. Shelly and I taught them early the Lord's Prayer, which at times became a comedy routine when they would recite it back to us. We taught them early that they should always talk to God confidently and that He listens, especially to young children.

Prayers at night were deliberate as well—not just memory words. We would pray for our family, brothers, sisters, and the baby in Mommy's belly. We would pray for the safety and success of all the police and special agents as well as our extended family and then thank the Lord for blessing us with the things we had: a house, a car, toys, and a good family.

There were many nights I could not be there for dinner or bedtime prayers. Sometimes I was not there for days at a time because of my profession. I recognized how important dinnertime was as a family and have read the studies about the positive impact this has on children. In reality, that was just not possible during my years as a street agent. I refused to let it haunt me as being something less than a good father. I believed it wasn't about the amount of time I spent in the arena. In that early season, it was the quality of the time I was willing to spend fighting for their hearts and minds.

As a result of being away at times, the kids quickly learned to ask the Lord to protect and bless Daddy as he went after the bad guys. And often when I did get home, I was routinely met by smiling, cheering kids. Don't get the idea that we were some perfect little Christian family. We struggled a great deal early on as many young couples with young children do. Financially, emotionally, and spiritually, we were always trying to find the right balance in dealing with all of these issues. In addition, any wife or husband who has to raise and care for the kids while a spouse is away for weeks or longer recognizes that it's not easy and can lead to monumental frustration and loneliness. If Shelly was ever frustrated, she never let it show. She always leaned on her amazing faith and spoke positively about me and my profession, often telling the kids as well as others who asked that my profession was a calling and that she was proud of me.

I am hopeful that, by now, readers recognize that our Christian faith was and still is the bedrock of our foundation as a family and as individuals. Shelly and I knew that all of our battles in the arena would be for nothing if our children did not come to a relationship with the Lord. Even then, they would not be immune to all the problems and temptations that a corrupt world offers. That is why we were motivated to find a great church where we could be fed individually and as a family.

We found such a church in West Covina. Going to church became a family outing and not a chore as is sometimes depicted. The kids soon loved the children's ministry, and Shelly and I were refreshed and fed every week by the teaching that was presented by the pastoral leadership. We would often talk about the lessons that the older kids learned at church and worked to build on them when we went home or at night right after prayers. Reading them stories at night about Bible heroes was special, and they all looked forward to it—not just because of the story but because Mom or Dad was spending time reading with them.

As the years went by and the kids transitioned from kindergarten to elementary school, we wanted to make sure that they began to see going to school as a positive activity rather than one that is detested. Shelly and I came from two different backgrounds when it came to education. Shelly loved school; she loved high school and college and excelled in every academic course she took. She has a keen logical mind as evidenced by her degrees in math and computer science. The harder the course, the more Shelly enjoyed and delighted in the challenge.

On the other hand, I don't know how I graduated from high school. I don't remember really doing anything in high school with the exception of playing some football and wrestling, and I was a mediocre athlete at best. For whatever reason, I despised school and hated going every day. It may be due to the fact that I don't remember any teacher who had any kind of an impact on me. I am in no way blaming the schools or teachers. It's just that I never had any interest in school, and that was problematic for me.

The only real memory I have is of a high school history teacher stopping my sister and me in the hall and saying, "You Capras will never amount to anything!" If I could have, I would have taken a chair to his head, but then I would have to answer to my father, which would have been a fate worse than anything else.

My father never placed much emphasis on education. His emphasis for his children was on our work ethic, respect, and dignity toward others, our word as honorable people, and our faith. I would learn years later that he would often say to my mother, "Someday they will realize that they are not stupid!" He was right. It took me some years to obtain my undergraduate and graduate degrees, but I did so with distinction and honors.

One of the benefits of attending college a little later in life was that no instructor or professor ever intimidated me. As a matter of fact,

I had a reputation for challenging instructors on their philosophical and ethical positions regarding any number of issues—and I did so with a great deal of respect and success. My experience convinced me that there are many teachers, regardless of where they taught, who did not have all the answers. Some could not be trusted with teaching the truth. I would also have contact with some so-called teachers who absolutely believed that only they—and not the parents—were capable of educating children. I believed it was important for our children who were preparing to enter school to understand that teachers were not to be feared, and sometimes they could be wrong.

During a break from a surveillance operation in West Hollywood in August, I located a school supply store to buy some materials to hang on the kids' walls at home. In particular, I was looking for cardboard alphabet cards that I could place around the borders of the kids' bedrooms. In addition, I found a model of the solar system that could be hung from the ceiling. As a visual learner, I believed these items—as well as others I found—would assist Shelly and me in helping the kids as they learned about a host of subjects.

While waiting in line, it became apparent that many of the customers were teachers as were the employees of the store. As I got to the checkout counter and placed the items down, my police radio crackled with a brief conversation between two units on the street. The gentlemen behind the counter looked inquisitively at me, cocked his head, and said, "Where do you teach school at?"

I smiled and told him that the items were for my kids at home. While rolling his eyes and with a look of derision on his face, he exclaimed, "Oh, another parent who thinks he is a teacher!" It took everything in me not to grab him by his ponytail and pull him across the counter where I could discuss my educational expertise. That sort of behavior was and is frowned upon by my outfit, and I really loved my job. I left the store thinking about the incredible arrogance of this individual, which solidified my opinion of some who were in the teaching profession. Regardless of how I felt, we raised the kids to be respectful to their teachers, school staff, and adults in general.

Raising our children to be respectful and truthful was a daily lesson as they grew. At the same time, we recognized that it was critical to help them develop an armor of confidence even before they went off to school. As far back as I can remember, we made a habit out of encouraging our children and telling them how proud we were of every accomplishment—no matter how trivial. Even things like learning the alphabet, tying their shoes, or learning how to write letters were always met with positive encouragement.

At the same time, if they failed at a task or a lesson, they would hear from both of us that failure was never final. We taught them and supported them and their ability to learn and achieve success. We did not want them to develop a fear of learning or trying new things. Our encouragement to them was more than saying, "Hey, kiddo. You can do it!" It was purposeful instruction as they developed their competencies from a very young age.

We encouraged their achievements and learned from their failures, and we also encouraged them by explaining that they were destined for greatness and that they were born for a moral purpose. We would often talk about their identity as Christians and as Capras. I would constantly discuss moral and character expectations with them that always dovetailed into their identity and purpose in life.

In my career, I witnessed so many young men and women who had no identity and no idea why they were here. They had no idea what they were born to pursue. They had no one pouring into their lives or fighting for them in the arena. Without an identity, a child grows up confused and has no idea what his or her true purpose is. They never develop healthy egos or a sense of pride. Instead, children who lack an identity are susceptible to being attracted to harmful activity such as gangs, drug use, and other unhealthy relationships where they learn to accept a twisted sense of purpose.

Often, I would tell my kids that when other people saw them or heard about them that they should expect to hear them say, "I want him on my team. I want to be in her class. I want to be connected to them." They should recognize that they were young men and women who were honorable, who could be counted on when things got rough, and who lived lives of purpose and direction. As the children's armor of confidence developed, they also developed positive attitudes and demonstrated courage and the ability to fend for themselves.

The ability for children to sometimes fend for themselves is becoming somewhat antiquated in our culture today. As a matter of fact, we seem to be in a time where we are intentionally raising a generation of weak-minded and fragile children who are so easily offended that they must be protected from hurtful words at all costs. As a result of our overreaction to the so-called bullying issue, these children have no idea how to stand for themselves. They have been so coddled by parents and/or institutions that they are not prepared for the brutality of life in the real world.

The evidence is clear, and one need only look at the recent college protests where some students are demanding certain college professors be terminated because their constitutionally protected statements had offended some students. In addition, some of those same students are demanding safe zones on college campus where bad words can't hurt them. How have children in this generation become so fragile and so brittle that a word or words actually cause them irreparable harm? I submit that one of the principal reasons for this is that we have become a fatherless nation. Our children are growing up in an emotional desert without the influence of a father. (I will go into this much further in another chapter.)

I firmly believe that another reason for the rise of fragile children is due to our attempts to minimize or stamp out bullying in our schools, which has birthed this unintended consequence. I am in no way disregarding the serious issue of school violence or the issue of bullying. However, even a CNN report stated, "Bullying, some researchers say, has been misused and abused in the last few years— too casually uttered about every hurt, slight, and fight, too frequently used in place of teasing or fighting."[6] This has led to an overreaction by schools and some well-meaning organizations that have decided that the children must never be exposed to having their feelings hurt. As an NFL quarterback once said, "Too bad there are no Band-Aids for hurt feelings."

Unfortunately, bullying has been thrown around so much that

the true meaning has become lost. That said, there have been bullies since the dawn of time; true bullies are nothing more than cowards who habitually utilize force, threats, or coercion to abuse, intimidate, or dominate others for pleasure or personal gain. Most bullies I have come across in my profession and in my personal walk have been pathetic, mean-spirited, weak-minded, selfish, self-absorbed cowards who are destined to be knocked off their pedestals.

There was a time in our culture when we openly accepted the notion that the best response to a bully was to have him or her smacked down. However, our current cultural climate shrinks back in horror when such a response is suggested because we are responding to the issue with violence. According to those in the so-called know, violence never solves anything except to beget more violence. This is not necessarily the case. There are moments when young boys and young girls will have to make the decision to defend and protect themselves from real harm from another child. To instruct or train a child to simply walk away from any conflict or run to the principal's office every time there is an issue will eventually erode the dignity of the threatened child, which ostensibly creates a fragile mind.

I can hear the screams of disbelief. "Are you saying we need to teach children to physically fight?" Absolutely—but more importantly, they need to be taught to be prepared to fight!

As the years went by, Shelly and I realized that it wasn't good enough for us to simply want to protect our children from any harm. We had to learn to empower them to act when necessary. In other words, we had to train and teach them that they had permission from us as their parents to aggressively act in the face of a conflict, in the face of evil, to protect themselves, to protect each other, or to protect others in need of assistance.

The girls and the boys were instructed to never to put their hands on someone in anger, however, if they were being accosted, bullied, or otherwise physically attacked by another student, they were permitted—and should—aggressively fight back until the attack was over. We taught them to use situational awareness when determining if they had to counter violence with violence. Are there multiple attackers? Is a weapon involved? Those situations would determine another course of action to remain safe. Regardless, they were told to never let the fear of detention or suspension keep them from fighting back because we would support the decision to defend themselves. I routinely encouraged the children to be willing to defend other students who were defenseless. I wanted them to be willing to step in and assist another student who was being accosted or bullied—or who was not able to fight back against an attack. I wanted them to act courageously when they witnessed injustice.

Micah played varsity football in high school. During his junior year, he witnessed two starting seniors holding a younger deaf student against the lockers, terrifying the young man. Micah was immediately enraged and pushed the two bullies back against the lockers and warned them both (using some choice words) that they should consider walking away. The seniors were initially shocked that a fellow football player was defending this young man, but a few choice words later, that was the end of any further bullying.

I have heard people say that it is better to be a "good witness" than to get involved in a physical altercation, but that is precisely the problem in our culture today. We are no longer conditioned to help others in need. Therefore, no one wants to get involved. Most people refuse to help others in need of assistance during a conflict. Why else is the popularity of the show "What Would You Do"[7] becoming so popular? The show deliberately sets up scenarios where a passerby witnesses a situation that would require an intervention, yet many people stare and walk away. It may be due to fear of harm, litigation, or something else, but I suspect if they were honest, the passerby would simply say, "It's not my problem."

What was true for defending themselves in school was also true for anywhere else. I would drill into them over and over again that if someone attempted to abduct them, they would most likely be killed. Their only response was to immediately fight for their lives. I showed them how to use keys as a makeshift weapon, how to break a finger, how to bite, and where to strike someone. I taught them to attack with ferocity and scream and yell at the top of their lungs. They were told time and time again that if someone did get them in a car, they had to find the courage to jump out—even if the car was moving.

We had to make sure they understood that they had our permission and our expectation to fight anyone or anybody who threatened to hurt them or abduct them. While Shelly and I prayed constantly for the Lord's protection over our children, I also made sure that I did my best to mentally prepare them to fight and win. Developing their armor of confidence was never just about their ability to do well in school. It has always been about the ability to be courageous and fight and survive in a fallen and corrupt world.

CHAPTER 3

PREPARING YOUNG MINDS FOR CONFLICT

In our walk raising six children, I often look back and realize that I, at times, was tougher on my children than many other parents were. Some of that toughness was misguided on my part—partly because I thought I had to raise perfect soldiers and partly because of the things I witnessed on the streets as a narcotics agent. As a matter of fact, several years ago, my oldest daughter came home from college for a short stay. After observing her little sister doing something, she quickly shouted, "Hey, Dad. I would never have been able to get away with that!"

I looked at her, smiled, and said, "You are right, sweetie. I am sorry. Daddy was a little stupid when he was raising you."

The other side of being tough was that I recognized the critical importance of instilling discipline in the minds of our young children. Often when I speak of instilling discipline, people immediately think in terms of punishment, which has nothing to do with the type of discipline I am talking about. Instilling discipline had to do with learning and demonstrating the rules of right behavior and conduct and recognizing that our actions result in consequences, both good and bad. As a narcotics agent, I daily witnessed the tragic lives of young men and women who came from broken and love-starved homes. At the same time, many of these lost souls were personally responsible for their tragic predicaments due to the poor decisions that ultimately led to fateful consequences. By the way, being tough while raising our children did not mean that as parents, we lacked love, empathy, or gentleness. Applying some toughness to training had everything to do with loving them and preparing them for battle in this culture by instilling habits of excellence.

Shelly and I wanted the kids to be friendly, but we also wanted them to understand the importance of choosing the right friends. All human beings want to fit in, be connected, and have relationships. I believe we are created for relationships—to be connected. However, some individuals want to fit in and be liked so badly that they will compromise their faith, moral positioning, and values in order not to be chided or seen as an outsider.

Children are notorious for being cruel to others who are different or who don't conform to the playground hierarchy. As parents, we fully understood and recognized that peer pressure is very real. We did our best to come up with creative ways to teach the kids about faith, discipline, moral behavior, and character development. Much of this was done through storytelling. Like most young parents, we read the entire Dr. Seuss library to our children as well as Mother Goose nursery rhymes. However, it was important for us to do our best to ensure that our children were aware that they were created for a great purpose and that they were destined for greatness no matter how long or how short their lives were on earth. We constantly reminded them that they were called to be set apart, not to just fit in or be a follower. They were called to be leaders and warriors who were constantly in training for the next season.

Starting at a very young age, I would utilize the life of a bald eagle as a metaphor for how each child was special and set apart. I would describe how the eagle may live in a community with other eagles, yet he does not flock. An eagle's eyesight is so great that he can see his prey or an approaching storm from over three miles away. An eagle doesn't eat rotting meat or have a relationship with birds that do. More importantly, an eagle's nest—his foundation—is so strong that it can weigh up to 1,200 pounds and withstand hurricane-force winds and provide protection for its young. One of the most amazing things about the eagle is how he faces an approaching storm. When a storm comes, eagles don't sit in their nests; in fact, they are known to step out on the edge of the nest and use the storm's winds to fly to heights far above the storm clouds. The eagles actually use the strength of the storm to help them rise above it. The eagle knows he will be bounced around in the storm, but he is confident that he was made to face the storm and withstand anything the storm brings.

Amazingly, throughout all our transfers around the United States, the kids attended public schools that all had the eagle as their mascot! In addition, I was able to develop a story utilizing the eagle as a main character, where a little boy learns the importance of building personal discipline, faith, and character in the face of life's greatest challenges. Almost every year, including their high school years, my kids would ask me to share the story with their friends or sports teams. (The story is now a book titled *The Eagle and the Seagulls: A Wisdom Story for Children and Adults*.)

Understanding that the children had an identity was another critical aspect of their growth. Knowing your identity leads one to find his or her purpose in life, so it was important to help shape their identities as Capras and as young Christian men and women. One of the ways we would reinforce the fact that the Lord designed each of them for a great purpose was to remind them of Jeremiah 29:11: "For I know the plans I have for you says the Lord, plans for good and not for evil, to give you a future and a hope."[8] We often incorporated this scripture into our prayer time in order to consistently remind them that each of them was unique and were created for a great moral purpose. We also encouraged them to identify the gifts that God had given them and reminded them that sometimes those gifts took time to manifest in their young lives.

Training up the kids was in no way a biblical boot camp. Instilling pride in their name and their faith should not be confused with moral superiority or familial arrogance. Shelly and I did not have a book, a manual, or lesson plans we followed each day. We simply recognized that the children needed to be poured into with love, discipline, truth (that sometimes was painful), and moral confidence in order to be prepared to face the secular and morally relative culture. We would often tell them that they were called to be examples of who they were and what they believed based upon their daily actions. I would tell them that others should look at them and say, "I want them on my team. I want them in my group. I want them as a friend." It was not because of some moral superiority. It was because they represented honor, character, excellence, and caring about the welfare of others.

Although we would continue to pour into our children in terms of our expectations of them while providing teachings based on our Christian worldview, they were each very capable of making wrong and selfish decisions. Even though we knew our kids were fantastic, God-fearing children, we recognized that they were all very capable of committing the most heinous acts possible. This is because I am all too familiar with the sin nature of humans. I have come across countless individuals during my career who appear soulless, who have eyes like sharks, and have no conscience, regard for dignity, regard for justice, regard for life, or regard or care about the afterlife. They were or are someone's son or daughter. When you get to know them, there is a clear and often familiar pattern. There was minimal or no parental influence, no guide, and no active love. They had no identity and no purpose. No loving adult in the arena was fighting for their lives or giving them direction and ethical guidance. Others came from families just like ours, but the children made terrible decisions or selfish decisions that started them down a road of destructive and painful behavior and consequences. As a parent, when you realize this is a possibility, it drives you to continually pour into your child and to continually be on your knees to seek wisdom and guidance. It prepares you to ready the life ring if and when necessary.

One of the goals in training up our children was to have them understand that they were all destined for greatness and designed by God to pursue this journey with passion. Over the course of several years, I have had the opportunity to speak to dozens and dozens of young men and women in high school. I quickly realized that many have a twisted sense of what "greatness" is really about.

In our American society, evidenced through most media outlets, Hollywood, and even academic institutions, we have often defined greatness along the lines of individual power, influence, financial ability, fame, and prestige. We would often advise our children that there really is nothing wrong with pursuing any of that—as long as it is pursued by following godly, ethical, and moral standards. However, the evidence consistently shows that morality and ethical behavior play little significance—if any—when discussing or defining many individuals' pursuit of being "great" in our culture. It is not unusual to hear young men and women say, "I want to be famous!"

Chasing celebrity status and fame continue to outweigh pursuing a moral and ethical purpose in life. The reasoning is really quite simple: if you decide to follow moral and ethical laws, there must be a moral and ethical lawgiver (God, the first uncaused cause). If there is a lawgiver, there must be a standard by, which everyone—at all times and at all places—must follow. Based on this logic and reasoning, we must come to the conclusion that pursuing moral and ethical laws causes one to be accountable for his or her actions, thoughts, and deeds. Therein lies the problem for many: we don't want to be accountable! This is why atheism and agnosticism (God is not knowable) are becoming more and more popular on our college campuses, in Hollywood, and in other institutions.

The belief that there is no God and that morality and ethical behavior are just relative gives one an excuse for pursuing what would otherwise be considered immoral, unethical, and despicable behavior and lifestyles. They may do so without being judged wrong by others because the behavior is morally relative. What's right for me may be wrong for you. There is no truth; therefore, I am not accountable for my actions. As a matter of fact, many young people who subscribe to this moral relativism are so completely offended by Christian principles and beliefs that they—along with their liberal college professors—continue to attempt to eradicate any form of Christianity on college campuses. It is the most selfish of beliefs that is narcissistic at best and ultimately leads to destructive consequences.

After watching a number of segments regarding the ongoing turmoil and cultural climate on American college campuses, a close friend e-mailed me and asked, "What happened to America?" I told him that I really believe we are entering a season where men and women of faith, character, and believers of American exceptionalism are being called out of the shadows to take a stand on what is right. Those things made this nation great and blessed. We are in desperate need of an American revival in terms of telling the truth about the greatness of this country. Over the past ten years, many good men and women have been pushed back into the shadows due to the PC culture that is destroying our liberty and freedoms by slowly chipping away at the very foundation of our Constitution.

We are beginning to reap what we have sowed. We have raised a generation of snowflake children who are so fragile and easily offended by everything and everyone, and it somehow has become the new norm. They march around campuses and communities, demanding that certain speech, dress, and even thoughts should be criminalized and/or outlawed. They are ignorant and unwilling to understand or learn the basic tenets of those inalienable rights given to us by God,—not the government—and subsequently codified by the founders of this great nation. They are motivated by liberal progressive thinking, which has become their "religion," and they worship on the altar of moral relativism. Unfortunately, instead of calling them out on it and pushing back, we have a number of leaders in public service, state and federal government, academia, and business who are quick to apologize in this politically correct culture for anything and everything that unnerves this spoiled, self-consumed, weak, arrogant group of pathetic young cowards! These same individuals are not willing to enter the arena. Instead, they enjoy mocking others from the safety of the bleachers outside the arena, which has become their pulpit.

We are reaping what we sow as we continue to witness the rise in a generation of men who don't know what it means to be men. We have lied to a generation of women by telling them they can have everything they want with little or no sacrifice. Why is this becoming the norm in our culture? Where have these young people developed these perverted ideas? Surely this is not just the fault of liberal, atheistic college professors. Much has to do with the lack of accountability taught at home and the overwhelming societal approval of moral relativism.

Nearly half of the children born in this great nation are born to single moms, yet this doesn't faze us as a people because we have simply accepted that this fact is not a problem in our society. As a matter of fact, there are many in the media, Hollywood, and liberal, progressive organizations who continue to laud single-mother households while crying out that men, husbands, or any other male partners are no longer necessary to raise a child. In some groups, the fatherless rate is as high as 75 percent, and there are many who want to blame the government, religion, the police, the founders, or any other number of scapegoats to shift the responsibility to others and away from personal responsibility. This is where moral relativism gets us. If it feels good do it. There is no right and no wrong. One plus one can equal three!

My wife and I knew that if we did not do our best to train up our children in the ability to think critically and with reason regarding their personal Christian faith and their moral beliefs, they might be highly susceptible to being influenced by perverted logic that could have the propensity to cast serious doubt on their walk. It was not so much that we feared they would question their faith and beliefs, which is, I believe normal at times. It was to prepare them enough that they would never be so utterly confused or seduced by emotional positions that they would abandon their faith altogether. Having an emotional response to our faith was important, but being able to articulate a simplified intellectual understanding of our biblical beliefs was important too. At the same time, it was very challenging for young children to wrap their minds around.

The Easter holiday at our home was a big deal. As a matter of fact, when the kids were young, Easter was almost like a second Christmas. We never did the Easter bunny thing, but we were not so legalistic as not to have colored eggs, candy, or other goodies on that day. We were intent on celebrating the life, death, and resurrection of Jesus Christ. I came to a point one year where I realized what a hard concept this might be for the kids. When they were young, they accepted everything that Shelly and I taught them. I wanted to try to make a little more sense of Easter—something that might be a little easier to understand for their young minds.

Following some research in the Old Testament on the Day of Atonement, I called all the kids into the living room and asked them to go get a bunch of their action figures, plastic animals, and some Legos. They raced back and placed them all on the table and laughed and kept asking what I was going to build. I began to set up a fort with the plastic logs and Legos as walls. I placed twelve action figures inside the walls, all separated by sections. Each of the twelve also had a plastic animal by its side. In the front, I positioned another action hero, which was Superman, Spiderman, or Batman, and then I carefully placed a plastic lamb at his side.

After setting it all up, I purposefully leaned back, looked at each one of my kids briefly, and started to explain what I had done. Pointing to each action figure, I explained that when the Lord gave His laws to the people, He set them up in twelve different tribes. Each tribe had a leader, like a pastor, who took care of the people in that tribe. While pointing toward the action figure at the front of the fort, I explained that the Lord appointed another pastor who was in charge of the other twelve pastors. I grabbed the figure at the opening and pretended to walk him and his lamb in front of all the other figures in the fort.

I explained that every year the main pastor would select a perfect new lamb with no flaws or birth defects. He would travel to each tribe, and each tribal pastor would place his hand on the lamb and ask the Lord to remove the sins of his tribe and put them on the lamb. The main pastor did this for every single tribe and then took the lamb to a rocky place and killed the lamb. He asked the Lord to accept the lamb as an offering in order to forgive all the sins of the people.

After a few seconds, I would explain that this is what Jesus did for us. The story became very understandable for the kids as they continued to grow. In fact, the story became a major part of our Easter celebration for years. We believe that, as Christian parents, it was our duty to assist them in growing in their faith. We never shied away from tough questions, and there were some questions that were difficult to explain. However, helping them believe and understand our faith was not about making theologians and/or Christian apologists out of them by the time they left high school. It was to provide some basic building blocks about why there is reason to believe in a loving and just God who designed us for a moral purpose.

During the last year of high school, I would remind them that everything they knew to be right and true—everything that they were taught about right and wrong and their faith—was about to be tested when they went off to college. I would tell them that they would be exposed to brilliant professors who would openly mock the Christian faith and anyone who believes in God. Those same instructors would posit positions and principles that sounded right in their heads, but in their hearts, they would know that it was a false position. I told them that, at times, they would not be able to counter these arguments due to their intellectual immaturity—but not to be afraid when faced with the issues. I advised them not to fear their inability to sometimes respond and to become experts in the professor's position so that they would be adequately prepared to respond effectively someday with love and compassion.

CHAPTER 4

ESTABLISHING RITES OF PASSAGE

As Shelly and I look back at our walk raising our children, we sometimes laugh at the expectations that well-meaning parents and other people would offer to us. Oh, you just wait until the terrible twos. Wait until the temper tantrums—when they start saying no and hitting and spitting. Wait until this or that or some other negative behavior that, according to them, was bound to manifest itself in our children as they developed.

Shelly would say, "No, we don't have terrible twos. We don't do temper tantrums or hitting or spitting." We didn't subscribe to whatever was being offered up as an expectation of future negative behavior. Those types of behaviors were absolutely unacceptable and were immediately dealt with so as not to form habits. We didn't consider how "cute" such behavior was since it would only encourage more of the same. Rather, our position and parenting strategy was that our children would develop habits of excellence—not control of us as parents or the household. I am not suggesting that our children were perfect little soldiers who did not push the envelope, but we would not tolerate unruly behavior, speech, or conduct starting at an extremely early age. Quite frankly, most of what other parents or people told us regarding expectations of negative behavior by our kids when they were very young never came to fruition because of our purposeful conditioning of their behavior—and not the other way around! Again, our primary purpose was not just to have well-behaved children. We wanted to develop morally grounded young men and women of faith who were destined for a grand purpose in this life.

When I speak of developing morally grounded men and women, I am referring to ensuring that the children developed belief systems as the cornerstones of their character, starting at a very early age. Character is really nothing more than the execution of one's beliefs. That is why someone's outward visible actions can lead us to determine whether they are a person of good or bad character because their actions are evidence of their character. Our hardwired beliefs lead us to what we value, and they are unseen or invisible unless we are asked. Our actions, visible conduct, and behavior are evidence that demonstrates whether or not we actually execute or put into practice what we really believe and value.

What we believe and why we believe in terms of our faith, moral positioning, how we should view the secular world, and how we should respond to others were lessons that were taught as enduring truths regardless of the season or the climate of the culture. I would often remind the children that they are constantly in training, preparing for the next season of their respective lives. In fact, we often made moving from one season to the next a "rite of passage," which was celebrated in different ways.

We started with something as simple as going from kindergarten (our kids never attended preschool) to first grade. This accomplishment meant the child would get his or her own backpack, pencils, paper, and a real lunch box. It was a big deal, and we made it into a celebration. The evidence that it was a big deal was the new school supplies they would be responsible for. This accomplishment came with a higher level of responsibility and importance for the child, and the rite of passage was getting new tools to go to school in this new season.

In a family of six children, these rites of passage set in motion a level of expectations for the younger siblings that motivated them to do well and look forward to the event. Often we would hear a younger brother or sister claim, "When I get to first grade, I get my own backpack and my own pencils." What was more amusing was to hear the first-grader tell a four-year-old or three-year-old how he or she wasn't grown up enough to have their own backpack yet because it only comes when you get to go to first grade. For little minds, this actually produced a sense of excitement and anticipation for school as well as the sense of "growing up."

We did our best to come up with basic rites of passage as a result of their accomplishments throughout elementary and middle school: a club sport, a school sport, your own calculator, or school trips. We always attempted to set in motion a positive expectation for the next season in their young lives. However, not every rite of passage was met with the same level of enthusiasm and expectation.

One of my closest friends and partner of seven years on the street sat with me one morning and asked, "Do you talk to your kids about, you know ... everything?"

I understood that he was asking if I talked to the kids about sex, intimacy, love, hormones, and all the other uncomfortable things that parents sometimes avoid because of awkwardness. "Yes, absolutely. Sex, drugs, and rock and roll. It's one of my favorite topics to talk about with my children!"

He looked at me, puzzled, and asked how I did it.

I told him that Shelly and I always believed that it was our responsibility to talk to our children when we thought they were ready for the subject. I told him the same thing I have told others: If we don't talk to them about it, if we don't discuss the godly beauty of attraction, they will ultimately hear it from their friends. Most likely, it will be explained in a twisted or perverse way. Discussing sex, intimacy, and relationships with our children was never taboo. We would not sit around hoping they would understand the significance of the subject matter by osmosis. We had a duty and a moral obligation to discuss these topics. Even if it was uncomfortable for the kids, it got to be known in our house as "The Talk."

I decided that somewhere around fourth grade was the magical time for discussing the topic of sex with the children—probably because I vividly remember my fourth-grade classmate trying to explain the graphic details of sex to me under the monkey bars during recess. I remember being absolutely repulsed and thinking, *This can't actually be how babies are made. There is no way my parents had done that!* It would be another year before my brothers and sister were summoned to the table to be read a book by my father on how babies are born. Following the story, my father simply stated, "And that's how babies are made." I was still horrified.

The purpose of the discussion would hinge upon the fact that the Creator of the universe designed males and females to be attracted to each other physically, emotionally, and sexually—for procreation and for enjoyment within the confines of marriage. The challenge I had was talking about the subject in a way that explained the godly significance and beauty of intimacy while minimizing the discomfort of the subject by avoiding any sense that the topic was dirty.

Usually I would say to Shelly that I thought it was time to talk to the child about sex. Having six children gave me the opportunity to get better at explaining and discussing the subject matter with the children. I made it a practice to approach the topic while I was driving or actually doing something active with the children when it was their turn for "the Talk." I routinely started by boldly asking, "Do you know what sex is?"

I could see it in their eyes! It was like a sledgehammer to the head! Although the conversation was usually a one-way discussion, which could last for up to an hour, I made it a habit to stop from time to time to ask if they understood or had any questions. I never did get a question, and the only response was a head nod. None of the kids looked forward to that particular rite of passage. I will never forget coming back from a drive with my youngest daughter after the Talk. I overheard her say to her oldest sister, "I can't believe it. Daddy just gave me the Talk!" Her oldest sister laughed and exclaimed, "Ha! You got the Talk!" My youngest daughter turned to her youngest brother and said, "Just wait until it's your turn to get the Talk. Ew!"

Although the Talk was initially uncomfortable for the children, we constantly reminded them as they prepared to enter high school about the importance and significance of godly relationships and intimacy. We often reminded them to honor themselves as well as other young men and women and avoid falling prey to the lie that sexual activity is really no big deal because everyone is doing it. I would explain to the children how we are constantly doing battle that takes place in our minds because our flesh can be weak and we often want to just allow ourselves to simply give in to our base desires.

I would also remind them that they must be ready to face the challenges of peer pressure as well as their own sexual desires, which are normal desires for human beings. I would often talk about how life brings consequences to our actions—both good and bad. They were always reminded that the Bible says that God wants us to live an abundant life. Part of an abundant life is not living a life filled with regret, guilt, or shame. We would remind them that sex was more than just a physical, feel-good act. It is a sacred act that connects individuals physically, emotionally, and spiritually. It is not surprising that when some men and women finally find their future mates, they often must deal with the regret of their prior sexual conduct, which may cause emotional pain but can also be overcome.

Entrance into high school has always been a big deal in our family and was met with a very significant rite of passage. There were no off-limits topics with our children. Throughout their high school journeys, there were times when it was necessary for Shelly and me to be in their faces—and in their spaces—about a host of things, including confronting foolish thinking, poor attitudes, undesirable conduct, and reestablishing our authority as parents.

Throughout my career, I have witnessed time and time again where children from all walks of life enter high school and slowly start to pull away from their parents physically and emotionally. I have concluded that some of this distance may be due to hormones, the transition into puberty, and the desire to become more adult-like because they are still trapped in a child's mind and body.

The other significant impact is the influence of others, including peers and older students. Let me assure you that *parents*, not peers, have a greater impact on decisions made by children during their youth! Studies indicate time and time again that parents who talk to their children and are engaged with their children more often have children who are exponentially less likely to be involved in toxic activities. Unfortunately, when some children pull away emotionally and physically from their parents, many parents begin to pull back at the same time, believing that the child needs to have room to develop his or her own identity and purpose. This often leads to a loss of communication and strained emotional relationships, which exacerbate the issues at hand. It is precisely at this critical time that the children need active parents who are engaged in their lives as mentors for direction and advice—whether the children want it or not!

For several months prior to my oldest entering high school, I struggled with how to develop a rite of passage that would make an impact on her. I had spoken to a number of other parents who had given their daughters and sons so-called purity rings with the promise to remain pure in their sexual conduct prior to marriage. I thought this was good, but I really wanted to do something more to remind her how special she was and how she was destined for greatness and not to be afraid of the challenges that would come during her high school tenure.

After much thought and consideration, I decided to simply write her a personal love letter from her father. After penning the letter, I placed it in an envelope and gave it to her along with a ring prior to her first day of high school. Writing the letter had a profound emotional impact on me. I realized that I would soon have to let my little girl go off into a fallen world. I questioned my effectiveness as a father. Am I preparing her to thrive and survive? Am I giving her the proper life skills? Have I provided her a foundation of faith? Have I been a good example?

I didn't realize the impact it had on her until I saw that she hung the letter up in a frame in her room for all to see. The moment I saw the letter on the wall, my doubts about my parenting efforts were somewhat diminished. It was as if she hung the letter to tell everyone, "This is what my daddy thinks of me. This is because he loves me!"

I decided that each daughter would receive a similar letter and a ring prior to entering high school. My youngest daughter gave me permission to use the following from the letter I gave to her prior to entering high school. The letter captures the essence of all of the letters I wrote to my daughters.

> Well, it's here, high school. What an adventure you are about to embark on! This is a very special time for you—a time to make new friends, to study new subjects, and to be exposed to new challenges. I am very proud of you, Rissy! You are a very strong, confident, and passionate young lady. You have a great capacity to love and care about not just your family but the well-being of your friends. You have an incredible gift to put into words your feelings as well as the ability to write stories. Those are gifts uniquely given to you by God—not only for enjoyment but also that they may be used to bless and comfort others. Take time to pray and ask the Lord to help and guide you in order to perfect and build on these gifts and talents so that His will be done in your life and the lives of others you impact.
>
> As you begin your journey through high school, you must be very wise about who you spend time with and who you will call a friend. You see, Rissy, there is great evil in the world, an evil that so despises our Creator that it will do anything to cause pain to His creation. High school is a glimpse of what is in the world. You are a part of His creation, and you must be prepared for temptations both great and small! You prepare by spending time with God, alone, talking to Him, asking Him for strength, for wisdom, and for courage. In other words you must do your best to be spiritually fit. This is not about being a perfect person because there is no perfect person except for Jesus Christ. This is about having an ongoing relationship with the heavenly Father, who loves you and knows you by your name, and above all, wants you to have an abundant life. Part of having an abundant life is

being free from the guilt of bad decisions we make, but even if we do, He is quick to forgive us. Never forget that Jesus died for you, that he shed His blood for the forgiveness of your sins, and nothing can separate you, Marissa, from the love of our God!

As you go into this new school year, you will be faced with sometimes very real decisions that have the consequences of life or death. And so, my daughter, I give you this ring as a reminder to make the right decisions; to be pure in your heart, pure in your thought life, and that each day you choose good over evil, peace over strife, forgiveness over hatred, comfort over despair and above all, life over death! I love you so very much!

Love,

Daddy[9]

Even now, when I rewrite this letter, I find myself reliving the emotions of the time. For my boys, I knew a letter would not do. I decided that their rite of passage would be to talk to them about the responsibility of being a man of honor, integrity, and character. I told them that they were destined for greatness and that they were born for a great moral purpose in this life—no matter how long or how short their time here on earth was. They were each called not to perfection but to pursue excellence and to be the example for others and that they served a just and holy God who loves them and knows them by name. They had heard me tell them this over and over in their young lives, but on this occasion, it was deeply and profoundly personal and passionate. I gave each one of them, at their appointed time, a gold cross and chain to wear around their necks in order to remind them that nothing they do would ever separate them from the love of our God. Our talk was always followed by a warm hug and letting them know how proud I was of them.

As the children had their moment, their particular rite of passage, their one-on-one talk with their father, I often became deeply moved in my spirit as I spoke with them. I remember praying and asking the Lord regardless of my own faults to let what I had to say stick in their hearts and minds. There is a great passage in proverbs that says: Train up a child in the way they should go, and even when they are old they will not turn from it.[10] I understood that this passage did not guarantee they would not have struggles, failures, or shortcomings, rather, in the fullness of their time, they would not completely depart from their training. These rites would reinforce their ongoing training as well as our beliefs in how we were to live our lives, and we hoped that the children would really understand and recognize their significance. I would soon be very moved to find out that my son wanted to establish his own rite of passage, which would be handed down to his brothers.

Turning eighteen was a big deal in our house for the kids, especially for the boys since they were required to sign up for selective service for the armed forces. Since his freshman year in high school, my son had his heart set on attending a military academy. By his senior year of high school, Doug had received two congressional nominations to attend the US Naval Academy. He waited every day to see if he would be granted an appointment.

A few days before his eighteenth birthday, Shelly asked him what he wanted to do on that day. Without hesitation, he simply said, "Mom, the only thing I want to do for my birthday is to have a cigar and a drink with Dad."

I was somewhat at a loss for words, but at the same time, I was so very honored that this was how my oldest son wanted to spend his birthday celebration. We celebrated by making a pitcher of daiquiris and smoking some premium cigars in the backyard of our home in Florida. I still have a picture of us puffing on the stogies right before he started to turn a little green around the gills and excuse himself for the night. His desire to be with his father on that day set in motion a new rite of passage for my other sons. Mark and Micah each celebrated their eighteenth birthdays with me in similar fashion, discussing their futures and destinies as men of faith and purpose.

These particular rites of passage were by far the most anticipated by our children as they excitedly looked forward to the moment we would challenge them to pursue greatness throughout high school and beyond. They would be faced with challenges as they struggled to make decisions that would impact their character, their faith, and their journeys into adulthood.

CHAPTER 5

TEACHING AND LEARNING
ON THE HOME FRONT

As Jim described earlier, I absolutely loved high school and college. My mother and father were strong proponents of academics and constantly pushed all their children to do well in school. I realized very early on that I had a talent for math. I loved the logic and challenges to solve problems. My father was a career IBM employee who loved his job and routinely spoke very highly of the company. He encouraged me to pursue math and computer science as a major in college, knowing that it would be the way of the future and would make me more marketable in the workforce. I took his advice and pursued a major in mathematics and a minor in computer science. I worked in the campus computer lab, leaving each shift with a new story. It was the late seventies, and I had to deal with the stress and turmoil of utilizing small computer card decks by the dozens as well as printing reams of paper from failed Cobalt programs.

For my senior thesis, I had the fortunate opportunity to instruct a group of adult learners who needed a refresher course on their mathematical skills in order to qualify for advancement. Although I was not interested in becoming a teacher, I discovered very quickly that I really enjoyed teaching math. The challenge was to do my best to make difficult and often boring subject matter exciting by really engaging with students and purposefully walking them through tedious steps in order to train them to think conceptually and logically.

I found that I never got frustrated by someone's inability to comprehend the mathematical process; rather, I took it as a personal challenge to ensure that by the time the semester was over, they would successfully pass the subject matter. By the time I graduated from college, I had been recruited and offered a position with IBM in their Poughkeepsie branch. A year after that, Jim and I would wed.

Jim and I spoke extensively about having a large family, which was something we both wanted. We would often tell those who asked that we were equally yoked in every aspect of our lives, which we would learn later is not always the case with a number of marriages. I always believed that a woman was the heart of a family, which meant that I had to do my best to pull the good out of any situation while applying discipline.

Raising six children meant my heart was involved in a lot of daily discipline. I continued to work after my first child, but in my heart, I wanted nothing more than to be a full-time mom. When I left IBM, we had one child and one on the way and were in the process of transferring from New York to Los Angeles. Our yearly income went suddenly from about $50,000 a year to $22,000, and both sets of our parents were more than three thousand miles away. Although it was quite an adjustment, we learned to live and thrive on Jim's income alone.

I have to smile when I remember being asked by a number of friends and others how we were able to live while having so many children, a mortgage, and other bills. I always said, "You just find a way and do it!"

Much of our "finding a way" meant we spent a great deal of time praying for God's help and blessing. As I look back throughout our family's growth, I can say without hesitation that the Lord never abandoned us in our time of need or our time of plenty.

I found out early on that being a stay-at-home mom had lost a great deal of the noble respect that it once held in our culture. It became apparent at the time that many women were starting to put off childbirth and child-rearing in order to pursue professional careers. I have always held that this decision is personal and must be left up to individual families and their given circumstances and beliefs. However, over the years, Jim and I have witnessed some women who openly despise and belittle the role of a stay-at-home mom as something not worthy of pursuing because it is allegedly highly sexist and "shackles" a woman to her husband and home. It's really quite a sad position to take and shows a complete lack of understanding of our commitment and selfless sacrifice for our children.

When our first child was born, we realized that life was no longer about us and about what we wanted. Everything revolved around the safety, health, and development of our kids. Our needs and wants became less than secondary in our lives. Jim has always held and said that there really is never any true success in life without some type of sacrifice. If we were to raise healthy, God-fearing, morally grounded children destined to make a difference in this world, we needed to be willing and prepared to sacrifice a number of things we previously took for granted.

Being a stay-at-home mom was really quite a misnomer for me since I was always on the go when the kids were very small. We were extremely fortunate that Jim was provided a government vehicle and we did not have to purchase a second car. Other than having a sick kid every once in a while, I made it a routine to load them up and head out almost every day. Whether it was going to the store, the car wash, or the park, visiting friends, or just driving around town, outings were an opportunity to teach. From colors to shapes to letters and numbers, teaching was constant and purposeful making as much fun as possible.

Our daily routine would shift as more kids were born and as the older kids prepared to enter school. Everything I did went around the kids and their schedules, including becoming an aerobics instructor and starting a class for toddlers called Fun, Jump, and Giggle. With so many little ones in the house, I found it impossible to afford extra activities for the kids. I started my own little business by sending out fliers and reaching out to churches and other recreational departments and civic groups. I was able to develop a program that was fun for children and very inexpensive for moms like me. Every time we moved to a new location, I would start from scratch and develop another program in that community.

Other than when they were in school, my children were with me every hour, including going to my own doctor's appointments. Though they were few, there were days when I was truly exhausted, especially when we had multiple kids under five and some in diapers. However, I never considered being a mom as anything less than a joy and blessing.

By the time the kids were in middle school and elementary school, I had developed a strict routine at the house. I would pick the kids up at their respective schools and then head home to have an after-school snack. Immediately after their snack—if there were no school sporting events—the children headed toward the homework room, emptied their backpacks, and produced schoolwork and assignment schedules. This was the designated area in the house, usually the kitchen table or the dining room table, where schoolwork was reviewed and homework and school assignments were completed.

I would do everything possible not to have schoolwork and/ or assignments considered a chore or a burden; rather, it was to be considered an integral part of the children's personal responsibility. Completed schoolwork, especially those that received high marks and/ or positive comments from teachers, was placed on the refrigerator or in a folder that Daddy would get to see when he arrived home. The importance of establishing and sticking to a strict routine was to develop habits that the kids would carry through high school and beyond.

Jim and I did our best, given our own academic abilities combined with his crazy work schedule, to be a team and assist the kids with their studies. Jim let it be known to anyone who asked that he did not do anything beyond third-grade math and science. Throughout our kids' entire academic careers, including college, I handled math and science and Jim handled reading and writing. Of significant importance to both of us was encouraging the kids to read, read, and read. I would tell the children that if they could read well, they could accomplish and learn just about anything. Often after nighttime prayers, they would listen intently as we read a variety of stories to them before going to sleep. As they got older, we would start to have them read stories to us as well as to their younger brothers and sisters and assist them when they got stuck on some word or sentence. Although we maintained a very strict bedtime schedule, we did allow those who were a little older and wanted to read in their beds at night to do so with their night-lights on. On many nights, I shut off night-lights and placed open books from their beds on a nightstand while they slept.

One of the really unique things as a mother of six children was discovering that although my children had many physical similarities, they each were born with distinct personalities and gifts. It became clear that, although they were all intelligent, they developed academically at their own individual paces. We were never concerned with the aptitude test scores that the kids had to take when they were very young regardless if they were high, medium, or low scores. We were confident that the children would ultimately do well as long as we continued to pour into their respective lives in order to develop character and academic ability. While I desperately wanted them to do well academically, it was much more important that they developed into young men and women of purpose who pursued the truth and their relationship with a just and holy God.

Our unified position regarding the overall worth (or lack thereof) of aptitude tests as well as the kids' academic development was one of the reasons we never enjoyed or appreciated parent-teacher conferences. We were often amused by how we were spoken to by some teachers: as if we were ignorant about training up our children. Jim actually despised going to the meetings, but he understood it was more important to our children and begrudgingly went when he was able.

We were summoned for one particular conference when our youngest daughter received a relatively low score on an elementary aptitude test. When we arrived at Ms. Smith's (not her real name) classroom, she had us sit down on the very small child chairs while she sat in front of us on her grown-up chair. She was a single, twenty-four-year-old teacher with about a year and a half in her position. She started out with the usual compliments of our daughter, which led to her attempting to explain how children learn.

Jim had just come in off the street after a long surveillance and looked somewhat disheveled and sported a few days of beard growth.

He started to do a slow burn, his jaws clenched, and he started to squint at her.

Ms. Smith began speaking to us very slowly and deliberately as if we may be having a tough time with the English language. I realize she may have meant well, but she was slowly walking herself into confrontation since she apparently thought we failed to recognize the significance of the standardized test scores.

Jim said, "We are not concerned about her scores!"

Ms. Smith looked puzzled.

Jim said, "Is she respectful? Are her homework assignments completed? Are there any behavioral problems?"

All of her responses were emphatically no.

Jim said, "Okay. That's all I am concerned about!"

By the look on Ms. Smith's face, it was clear she was distressed by our response.

I squeezed Jim's hand and said, "Thank you for your concern and time meeting with us. But just so you know, she is our fifth child of six."

Ms. Smith's eyes suddenly opened wide as she leaned back in her chair.

"Please understand that we have never been overly concerned with standardized test scores, and quite honestly, we are confident that she will do quite well academically—just like her other brothers and sisters."

As Ms. Smith stumbled for words, I could see that Jim was very aggravated by her demeanor. I squeezed his hand harder in order to keep him from losing it further, but it was no use.

Jim said, "One more thing, Ms. Smith. Just so you know, my wife has a math and computer science degree, graduating with high honors, after which she had a career with IBM. I hold a master's degree in education. Again, we are not overly concerned and are clearly comfortable with how she is progressing."

Ms. Smith became flushed and apologetic, bumbling over her words to try to minimize her young arrogance and assuring us she did not mean to be disrespectful.

I advised her that we understood her well-meaning concern and shook her hand and thanked her.

As we walked out of the school, Jim looked at me, shook his head in disgust, and said, "Again, another teacher who thinks parents are idiots!"

Over the course of raising our children, we have had a lot of positive interaction with the public school system and have met several wonderful and dedicated teachers in our journey. However, it has been our experience that too many teachers really don't know how to teach. Of course, they have their teaching certificates, which are held up authoritatively as evidence of their ability to teach, but a teaching certificate is worthless if one lacks the passion to be successful in the profession. For that matter, lacking passion will minimize anyone's ability to be successful in any profession.

During the latter part of our tour in Virginia, all six of our kids were in school full time. I was advised that the local school district was looking for a part-time ESL teacher (English as a Second Language). I applied for the position and was hired, but because I did not have a teaching certificate, I would be paid at a lower wage through the No Child Left Behind Act. In addition, my lack of a teaching credential meant that I would be prevented from applying for a full-time position. None of these issues caused me any concern. I was happy to have the opportunity to teach and receive some additional income.

The position was established to assist students with passing the Standards of Learning (SOL) exam, which was a requirement for moving to the next grade and for graduating from high school. I was advised prior to taking the position that most of the students were severely deficient from an academic position and that less than 40 percent of the students attending ESL classes passed the SOL tests.

While the initial information was negative, I saw it as a unique challenge to assist students who had families that came here seeking a better life for themselves. The opportunity to be an ESL instructor also provided me with the ability to teach our own children about how great and blessed we are to live in these United States. I would often ask them how they would like to suddenly move to a foreign country where people spoke another language, celebrated a completely different culture, ate different foods, and still expected them to succeed. That is precisely what thousands of families from around the world do each year in trying to come here to pursue a better life for their children. This provided a grand lesson in why we should respect and honor our heritage as American citizens.

Over the course of the next year and a half, I was able to develop a wonderful relationship with many of the students in the class. I assisted in their academic training and was able to assist some of them in receiving their driver's licenses, securing employment, graduating from high school, and moving on to college or other professions.

I was subsequently advised by some of the school staff that they had seen a dramatic improvement in many of the ESL students by virtue of the increase in their respective academic standing. I would often get asked where I taught before or where I received my teaching credentials. I said, "I don't have a teaching degree, and I teach like I teach my own children." I was routinely looked at with some skepticism or disbelief.

By the time we were ready to move to our next duty station, the passing rate for ESL students was above 80 percent. In a short period of time, I grew to really care for and love these young men and women. To this day, I receive letters and e-mails from a number of them who are now married and have families of their own.

We have always attempted to utilize our sometimes-mundane daily experiences as object or life lessons for our children. While I thoroughly enjoyed my experience as an ESL instructor, the opportunity also afforded me the ability to highlight the importance of making a positive difference in the lives of others. We would often discuss how chasing selfish desires or self-serving interests had no eternal significance and how individuals who become consumed with themselves and their own success may ultimately lose everything.

Treating others with dignity and respect was a highly placed value in our family. The kids were taught to speak to adults and those in authority with a distinct level of respect, and nothing else would be tolerated. That included how their young friends acted when they were at our home. On one particular occasion, a young boy attempted to call Jim and me by our first names. Jim immediately called the young boy over and told him he was not his buddy or pal and that when he came to our house, we were to be addressed as Mr. and Mrs. Capra. The boy said he understood.

Later that afternoon, my oldest son said, "That's a really bad kid!"

When I inquired further, he went on to say he used extremely harsh language and "talked about bad stuff." Some days later, we wound up sending the same young boy home again after he became unruly in the front yard. A few days after that, the boy's mother and her boyfriend came over to our house a little upset over the situation. As they began to cautiously explain that they were sure their son did not mean to cause any problems, Jim cut them off. Jim explained that he was very aware of their son's conduct and unacceptable behavior in the neighborhood. He further explained in a very terse tone that their son's conduct and behavior was their respective responsibility and not ours. However, when he came to our house, we expected him to behave in an appropriate way. If he couldn't, he was not welcome here. They both seemed a little taken aback, and after some further small talk, they got up and left. We never had any further contact with them or their son and were subsequently advised that they moved from the area about a year later.

By then, our children had already begun to develop a healthy sense of what our expectations were for them—and their friends. They began to understand how important it was to develop good friends who may come from different backgrounds and cultures but understood honor and respect. From time to time, we would listen in amazement as the older kids admonished their younger siblings to be cautious or to stay away from someone in the neighborhood due to unacceptable conduct and/or behavior. They were beginning to utilize wisdom in choosing their friends, and they were actively looking out for the welfare of their siblings. At every opportunity, we would remind them that they were called not to be sheep and merely follow others aimlessly. Their walk was for a greater purpose, and we started to describe them as warriors who were called to pursue excellence and were destined for greatness.

CHAPTER 6

SHINING A LIGHT ON THE LIBERAL TOLERANCE MYTH

Does truth still have a place in government? Does truth still have a place in business? Does truth still have a place in our communities and in our personal lives? Is truth really just relative? Can it be anything we want it to be? If so, where are justice, security, and social order?

Although truth has become relative to many in our culture, we have struggled to teach our children very simply that truth is most often used to mean in accord with fact or reality or fidelity to an original ideal or *standard*. We have often attempted to make them aware of how critical the search for knowledge is in their walk and to understand that knowledge often constitutes truth. If you no longer pursue knowledge or keep knowledge in the dark, you may never get to the truth.

According to Dr. Jim Dennison, we live in a culture that no longer has the necessary tools to determine right from wrong.[11] As a result of our postmodern society, we continue to witness the rise of a toxic anti-Judeo-Christian culture that worships liberal tolerance, which is grounded in relativism. In this climate, postmodernists rabidly exclude God from making any sense of reality and/or our human experience. They do not recognize any universal truth, reason, or morality. In fact, reasoning and logic seem to be pushed aside when postmodernists arrive at their amoral conclusions that there is no truth. There are only personal opinions, views, and perspectives.

Postmodernists believe and radically teach that liberal tolerance is more than just a view. It is held up as an absolute truth that no one point of view on moral and religious knowledge is objectively correct for every person at all times in all places. In other words, there is no truth—absolutely—because all views, ideas, and lifestyles are equally valid and none should be considered better than any other.[12]

One needs only to study that position briefly to see the comical absurdity of that statement. There is no truth except for the truth that there is no truth—can that be true? It is a self-defeating argument that is taught as gospel and is poisoning young minds by failing to have them think critically, logically, and with reason. Liberal tolerance is taught as the great so-called neutral position one must take in order to avoid offending others, but it is more than that. It is a corrupt philosophical way of living that is devoid of basic, good, moral principles of behavior. It is embraced as a way of avoiding any sense of accountability by positing that truth is relative and "what's true for you may not be true for me." Augustine wrote, "We love the truth when it enlightens us; we hate the truth when it convicts us!" Therefore, embracing moral relativism affords individuals the opportunity to suppress the moral voice of restraint to get what they want without conviction.[13]

We were never shy about reminding the kids that they would have the opportunity to meet other young men and women at school who were raised differently than our family. They wouldn't necessarily have a similar faith or similar beliefs in a number of areas, but that did not preclude those individuals from becoming friends. Even to this day, I caution the kids to be careful in criticizing others about how they live, were raised, or how they raise their respective children. They probably look at us and think we are the strange ones. The challenge was to have them understand that it was okay to disagree with someone's ideas and views.

As a matter of fact, just because someone was an acquaintance or a friend did not necessarily mean that you had to agree with his or her views. In addition, we told them to never feel pressured into agreeing with someone's views because it might end a friendship or a relationship (peer pressure.) Furthermore, they were instructed to always treat others—even those they disagree with—with dignity and respect and not their views or ideas. Tolerance has nothing to do with an opposing view; it has everything to do with how we treat and respond to the individual holding that opposing view. According to Gregory Koukl, "Tolerance is reserved for those we think are wrong, yet we still choose to treat decently and with respect. [14]

This is where the apostles of liberal tolerance vehemently differ. Again, liberal tolerance firmly holds that all views, ideas, and lifestyles have equal worth. Therefore, those who disagree with an idea, position, or lifestyle are immediately accused of disrespecting the person and subsequently branded as intolerant, racist, homophobic, bigoted, misogynistic, and/or a host of other labels in an attempt to silence those who hold a different world, theological, or moral view. Their ability to successfully utilize fear—I would define it as psychological terrorism—forces many to be silenced rather than facing public accusations that damage our collective reputations and safety as well as facing termination and/or civil litigation. It is, by all accounts, a cowardly tactic to avoid rational, reasonable, and logical intellectual engagement of any subject matter.

George Orwell said, "The further a society drifts from the truth the more it will hate those that speak it!" [15]

I have found myself incredibly mystified that there continues to be legions of well-educated men and women who affirm and teach that all views and all positions are equally valid and have equal merit. As a former federal narcotics agent, I have come in contact with some of the most notorious criminals on the face of the planet who have committed horrendous acts of terror on other human beings. It is clear that their views are dangerously unstable and severely psychologically flawed, and the executions of those views and/or positions have resulted in the tragic loss of life, liberty, and freedom.

Are we really to believe that these types of views are valid? If so, then it's all a matter of preference. We are incapable of determining the truth or—for that matter—what is right and wrong. I am suggesting that this is what many so-called liberal progressives want to promote. If we take this idea to its illogical conclusion, we then are incapable of stating that radical terrorists who skin others alive because of their religious beliefs are wrong. It's a matter of preference, and their views are valid! Yes, it's insane and comical at the same time! We live in a country that honors freedom and liberty, yet freedom and liberty demand responsibility and a moral code of conduct that we hold up as a standard. When you take liberal tolerance and moral relativism to the brink, you realize that there is no standard at which point social order begins to disintegrate.

We were well aware of the reality that if and when our children voiced their Christian worldview in the public square—at school or other functions—it could result in being marginalized, being humiliated, or being an outcast. We encouraged them to respond confidently, courageously, and with humility. We would remind them to love people where they were and not find any joy in what they considered false views, false ideas, or the shortcomings of others. If we respond to false ideas, views, and/or moral positions, we should do our best (as difficult as this is) to model what Jesus did and taught during his ministry.

Jesus, throughout his ministry, never poked anyone in the eye for a sin or ostracized anyone for immoral behavior. He loved them right where they were, always forgave them, and let them know He had a better way for them to live. He was often accused by Sadducees and Pharisees (the politicians and lawyers) of keeping the company of sinners, tax collectors, and prostitutes. He would respond that a physician does not visit those who are well. He attended to the afflicted and those in need. Jesus spent time with them, ate with them, and loved them unconditionally. The only people he admonished were the Sadducees and Pharisees who He called a "brood of vipers" for twisting the minds of those they were supposed to be shepherding.[16]

When asked which commandment was the most important, He answered that we should love the Lord your God with all your heart, soul, mind, and strength and then said that the second most important was to love your neighbor as yourself.[17] I had always found it easier to love my God rather than to love my neighbor. In fact, there were times I asked myself how I could love a neighbor I didn't like, but then

I realized He didn't command us to like them. He commanded us to love them as we loved ourselves.

We leaned on this scripture to explain to the children the importance of loving others they came into contact with—even those we disagree with on a number of views and ideas. This type of love was not a romantic love or a quiver in your liver; this type of love meant that they had to be willing to consciously care about others and be willing to unconditionally assist those in need. This kind of love would require them to put aside personal opinions, assertions, and feelings and act with compassion for the benefit of another.

The story of the Good Samaritan is a perfect illustration of this kind of love. What is often missed in the story is the fact that the Jews and the Samaritans hated each other for generations; that same hatred is still evident in the Middle East today. As a matter of fact, Bible scholars contend that their hatred ran so deep that the Samaritans and the Jews would often go completely around a town or city just to avoid coming into contact with each other. Yet here, in the story, Jesus tells us that the Samaritan had compassion on the man, bandaged him up, took him to a hotel, and paid for his stay. He let the innkeeper know he would be back the next week if the money was not enough. The Samaritan loved his neighbor and took care of him as he would have taken care of himself. The lesson is certainly easy to discuss, but in practice, it can be difficult to execute in a fallen culture.

We routinely encouraged them to be positive examples and light bearers in a dark world so that others who witnessed their actions and behavior might give them reason to be introspective and consider how they are living out their own lives. The life lessons we taught them were not so they would try to change a fallen culture. Instead, we hoped they would not let the culture change or conform them. "Do not conform to the pattern of this world, but be transformed by the renewing of your mind."[18]

This is the same way we approached our responsibility in considering the "great commission," which was to make disciples of the entire world. We often taught our children that the best way to do this was to be an example. We taught them to let their character and demonstrated behavior become their witness. I would offer that their friends and others may not be very receptive to a beating over their heads with a Bible, but they likely would be receptive of the example they provided in their everyday lives.

Once again, we were not attempting to create young theologians, apologists, or pastors. We wanted them to live out their faith and beliefs the best they could, fully recognizing that they would make mistakes, but that should never keep them from pressing on.

We are firm believers that men and women of faith should take an aggressive role when government legislators at any level attempt to infringe on the religious liberties of American citizens. I am not in any way suggesting that our sole responsibility is just to sit back and love those we disagree with, especially those in positions to change our laws. We have continued to train up our children to recognize that people of faith need to make their voices heard to those in power—and we should never shy away from that responsibility. As a matter of fact (and this will likely annoy some within our community), I believe that our country is in such a moral and ethical mess because the Christian church and people of faith have remained too quiet, relying on others to fight our battles—or simply relying on prayer.

In the heat of the Revolutionary War, George Washington admonished his soldiers to "trust God, but keep your powder dry" referring to the gunpowder they would need to fire their weapons at the enemy. [19]

The Christian community has power and influence when we come together collectively to push back and fight against repressive legislation as was evident in the recent defeat of a proposed bill in the California legislature. The bill would have threatened the religious liberty of all religious schools in the state that are not seminaries. It would have required that such schools not "discriminate" against LGBT students or lose federal funding, ultimately eliminating the religious liberty of all California faith-based colleges and universities. The California senate committee was inundated with calls and complaints, resulting in the proposed bill's defeat, ensuring that religious exemptions are kept in place.

I believe in the power of prayer, but I also believe that we must be willing to do battle and push back with ferocity when faced with legislation that cripples and marginalizes our religious liberties. At the same time, we must act with love and compassion with those who practice lifestyles, views, and behaviors contrary to our own walks.

Ever since she was three years old, my middle daughter Rebecca loved to sing. My wife and I noticed very early that she had a beautiful voice (we still don't know where that came from), and she was fearless when she sang in front of others. In middle school, she attended a talent show and brought the house down with a contemporary pop song. Becky is also a very devout young Christian woman with a sensitive, caring spirit. She has an absolute heart for the Lord and a gift for encouraging others in need. Following the leading of her heart, she applied and was accepted to college in Oklahoma, majoring in musical theater.

Months before she left for her first semester, I took the time to sit with her and explain how everything she was taught, everything she believed, and everything she knew was morally right would be tested. We had an opportunity to discuss how she would meet any number of people in the entertainment arena who lived completely different lifestyles. I remember looking at her and saying, "Love them, Becky, each one you come in contact with—no matter what their story, no matter what their beliefs, no matter what their lifestyle, love them like a friend." We discussed how she did not have to approve of their views and lifestyles, but she would be called to love them, pray for them, and encourage them to do well. I look back and realize that I never really had to have this conversation with her because this was Becky's gift; she was that way to everyone she comes into contact with.

A few years later, I received a phone call from Becky while I was in Washington, DC. After a few pleasantries, I could tell that something was on her mind.

She said, "Dad, something strange happened at rehearsal tonight ... one of the actors I know who is a friend approached me after rehearsal. He is a terrific actor and a singer who is also openly gay and extremely flamboyant."

I asked her what happened.

"Dad, he looked at me and said that he heard I was very religious. I told him that I didn't know about being religious, but I am a Christian."

"What did he say, honey?"

With her voice a little shaky, she said, "Daddy, he looked at me and said, 'Your God must hate me.' I looked at him and said, 'My God doesn't hate anyone. In fact, he loves you right where you are."

"Wow," I said. "What did he say?"

"Dad, he just looked at me a little sad and turned and walked away."

I assured her that her response was powerful, beautiful, and loving. I told her that I believed the Lord gave her that response for her friend. In fact, while I can't know this for sure, I told Becky that he might have never heard that he is loved. It is quite possible that he has endured insults and ridicule from those who claim to be religious individuals.

It would have been easier if she were to deny her convictions to avoid any confrontations regarding lifestyles, especially since Becky saw this young man on a daily basis. She never had any further interaction with him regarding her faith, but he had to realize that she was different because she was courageous enough to share her belief with love and compassion.

CHAPTER 7

A MESSAGE TO FATHERS

I stated from the beginning that this book would not be a how-to book. I wanted to share our walk, as fallible parents, in raising children of faith, discipline, and purpose. However, in doing so, we would be remiss in not sharing important facts regarding parenting studies and how the lack of an involved parent has a debilitating impact on a child.

Parenting is no simple walk regardless of your socioeconomic status. I have seen extremely wealthy children of two-parent households growing up as lost misfits, and I have witnessed impoverished children from single-parent families growing up to become pillars of society. And while we recognize that many children are growing up in single-parent households due to divorce, death, or other reasons, it does not automatically suggest that the child will live a life of crime or poverty. However, it does mean that the single parent raising that child alone has an exponentially harder challenge in rearing that child toward a successful future. Oh, and in case you were wondering, the divorce rate in the evangelical Christian churches is no different than the rest of American society!

I have been a warrior my entire life, and I have been incredibly blessed to have been given the opportunity to serve in that capacity for more than three decades in military service and as a federal narcotics agent in major cities around the country and in the international arena. Well over half of my career has been in leadership positions, and I have had the opportunity to speak and teach around the country about drug use and abuse, national security issues, and parenting and family issues to public servants and citizen groups.

In almost every lay group, I was asked, "How can we help you, Mr. Capra? How can we help? What do we need to do to help you?"

At first, I would say how much I appreciated the question, but over the course of time, I began to realize there really was a way for them to help—in a much more valuable way than what I was doing on the streets. I told them to go home and invest time, energy, and love to their families. I began to say, "If you really want to help me and the men and women of law enforcement, go home and jump into the arena and be a warrior for your family!"

On some occasions, it became obvious that some people in the audience did not want to hear that. They wanted to be able to sign a petition, give a donation, or pledge some type of support. It's easier than actually getting into the arena. Getting into the arena is work. Getting into the arena takes time. Getting into the arena takes sacrifice and can be risky. "Let me start out by asking you fathers out there a question. Are you a warrior at home for your family? Well, are you?"

As a nation, we have pumped millions of dollars into myriad programs in an attempt to keep young kids on the straight and narrow. Quite honestly, most have been abysmal failures. Any law enforcement officer will tell you the same thing: we have become a fatherless nation, and our children have no positive role models to emulate and/or provide ethical and moral guidance. The rise in fatherless birth rates continues to cast growing segments of our society into a perpetual spiral of destruction and poverty.

More than 42 percent of all the children born in the US are born to single-mother households. In black communities, that number is exponentially higher. We refuse to talk about this reality because it might offend someone's sensibilities. We have become so fragile and politically correct that we shriek in horror when the truth is told and demand that our collective minds be protected from such talk and such truth. Seriously, it should concern all of us. It's a travesty!

We are also witnessing a rise in absentee fathers. These fathers are living with their families but are disengaged from child-rearing responsibilities. (I can't tell you the number of times I interviewed young people involved in criminal conduct who told me they had no father or hadn't seen their father in years.) In both cases, where children fall asleep without a resident father and where resident fathers are not engaged in the lives of their children, those children are more likely to be involved in juvenile crime, poor grades, drug and alcohol abuse, and mental illness.

Children who grow up with healthy relationships with their fathers are more likely to succeed than those who do not. Children who have no influence or relationship with their fathers live in emotional deserts. I have read many articles by supposed child experts who have claimed that parents have little influence on their children. They claim that their peers have a greater influence on them. That is bull! Their peers will have an influence on them if their fathers are not pouring into the lives of their children.

The rise in crime and violence in the US is directly attributable to the disintegration of the American family, yet we hide behind race, poverty, and other excuses in order to avoid the truth. With no fatherly influence many young children have no identity. Without an identity, they have no purpose. They quickly fall prey to other twisted ideas and groups or gangs that provide a perverted sense of purpose and meaning in their young, vulnerable minds.

Many young men and women are desperately looking to fill the void in their lives that only a father can fill. Unfortunately, without a father, that void is often filled with wrong and hurtful behavior that has painful and destructive consequences. Roland Warren said it best, "Kids have a hole in their soul the shape of their dad! And if a father is unwilling or unable to fill that hole, it can leave a wound that is not easily healed!"[20]

The evidence consistently indicates that children who grow up without fathers or with absent fathers are exponentially more likely to be involved in crime or drug and alcohol addiction. They are more likely to drop out of high school. They have a higher risk of suicide, mental illness, teenage pregnancy, and lifelong poverty! We continue to lie to ourselves as a nation and say other things are responsible because that somehow passes the blame to the state or federal government, the police, the schools, or someone or something else. Rarely is there any discussion of personal accountability since it does not fit the politically correct narrative today.

Young boys need role models, mentors, and fathers to model what it is like to love your wife and show what being a man is really all about. Young girls desperately need a daddy's love and approval and direction, and they literally become emotionally lost and scarred without a relationship with a father.

I remember vividly each of my girls asking, "Daddy, do you think I'm pretty? Daddy, what do you think of this outfit? Daddy, do you like my hair? Daddy, will I find a man?" Children are desperate for a father or father figure to pour into them confidence, pour into them love, pour into them God's Word. They don't need perfection; they need a fathers' love.

No matter what your situation is, your children thirst and hunger for a relationship with you—even if that time is brief due to distance or any other reason. No amount of child support can take the place of an active father in the lives of young men and women. As a father, you have a God-given responsibility to walk into the arena of life and fight for the future of your children. Yes, it's difficult. Yes, it's demanding. Getting into the arena is work. Getting into the arena takes time. Getting into the arena takes sacrifice. Getting into the arena can be risky. You need to be a willing warrior for your children because they are waiting for you.

Unfortunately, in magazines, commercials, and television shows, men are continually depicted as feebleminded dolts who don't understand their wives or their children. They go about their lives as nothing more than mindless, sex-starved, beer-drinking fools who are completely disengaged from family life. This lie continues to be perpetrated by a number of so-called liberal progressive groups who believe that men are only necessary for procreative purposes—and even that is questionable. However, I would like to remind those fathers, those men who have an ear to hear, that all fathers have been designed to walk the warriors path. I submit that there is a tug on a man's heart to be a warrior. That tug, that drive, that calling to pursue the path comes from God the Father. His still quiet voice calls the warrior to the arena.

A father who takes his position as warrior recognizes that he is a man of purpose and a man of integrity. He willingly engages in a daily battle, cause, or conflict for the heart of his children. As Christians, I absolutely believe that men are called to do battle on behalf of their families. However, I do not subscribe to the notion that when we come to a relationship with Jesus Christ we somehow suddenly become part of the holy, happy, healthy, wealthy club.

I have had the opportunity to witness parents say and believe that if they take their kids to church, have them in small groups, and go to Christian-sponsored events, their children are going to be all right. That is wishful thinking because none of those things replace a father's active relationship with his children—no matter where they are, no matter what their age.

Men have a tendency to constantly compare ourselves to other men we come into contact with. We compare our looks, our schooling, our income, our effectiveness as husband and father, and on and on and on. We have a tendency to think how easy someone else has it or how put together another dad, husband, or family is compared to our own. During a speaking engagement at a men's ministry event, I jokingly told a group of men the following story:

> As I pull into the church parking lot, I look at the family getting out of the minivan ahead of us. Out walks the perfect little family all dressed impeccably well with matching outfits for their three boys: twelve, ten, and eight. The kids were all carrying their little personal Bibles as they walked in a perfect row toward the doors of the church. As I look at them carefully navigating across the rain-soaked pavement toward the church, I couldn't help but wish that the next car that drove by them would splash mud on them, praise the Lord. And as I look back trying to get my own crew of six

out of the car, I realize that one still has on his Ninja Turtle pajama top, the next one has one shoe on and no socks, the other one still has toothpaste on her face and is eating a pop-tart—and is that the cat in the oldest one's backpack?[21]

We need to realize that, as men, we are each called to walk our own walk. It takes us to our destiny as a father, a husband, and a leader. I don't believe for one minute that the Lord is looking for you to be a perfect parent or a perfect father because there are none. However, I do believe He is calling men to be willing to go to battle on behalf of your children, to begin a relationship with them, to love them, to discipline them, to pour greatness into their lives, and to let them know they were created for a great purpose. Hey, men, never mind about somebody else. Are you willing to be a warrior for your children? Your children have been waiting for you!

When I was growing up, my father was Pharaoh. I didn't speak back to him until my second year in the navy, and even then, I was a little scared! There were no hug fests or long talks in my house, but my father taught me more about honor, integrity, commitment, and work ethic than any book or police or military institution ever did. He never mentioned those words. He had a tenth-grade education, if that. He was far, far from perfect, but he always was and continues to be my hero in this life because he was willing to have a relationship with me and fight for me in the arena of life—even if it was only a moment. Hey, men, are you willing to be a warrior for your children and fight in the arena on behalf of them? They are waiting for you.

I often speak and teach on servant leadership. I routinely ask, "What is the number one reason employees leave their job?"

A lot of people instinctively think its salary or benefits, which is actually about the seventh reason people leave. The number one reason individuals leave is lack of self-worth, a lack of value, a lack of care or concern for individuals by the organization, and a lack of a relationship with the employer. The same is true in family relationships—whether they are parent to child or husband to wife. If there is a lack of self-worth, the individual will go find it from someone else. If you are not pouring life lessons into your child, who is? Where are they going for training, wisdom, and discipline? Who are they seeking validation from? Who are they receiving love from? Who is fighting for them in the arena? They are waiting for you!

Being in the arena prepares a father to lead, to love, to train, to discipline, and to be the example of excellence (not perfection). While you are in the arena, you are paving the way for your children and for your family. While you are in the arena, your children and your family are watching you—your every move, your words, your prayers, and your tactics. It is critical for your children to learn and understand that there is no real victory without a sacrifice. If you failed at times that they witness, that failure is not final—and that forgiveness and redemption could be found in the arena.

There are no perfect warriors in the arena. There are only men of purpose, action, and clear mission. If you are starting to count all the reasons why you can't get into the arena—you don't have time, your job is too demanding, and on and on—you are listening to the enemy's lies. You need to engage in the battle for your children and for your family. It is never too late.

As Christian men, we do not divest our responsibility to train up our children to the church, the state, or to anyone else. We are not called to be perfect, but we do need to be willing in order to make a positive difference in our children's lives. We only have a moment here in this life. Our life, as the Bible says, is as a vapor. What will your legacy be to your children—the next generation?

I will not be receiving the Jim Dobson Focus on the Family Father of the Year Award any time soon, but it doesn't keep me from fighting in the arena. God's promise in Jeremiah said, "For I know the plans I have for you says the Lord, plans for good and not for evil, to give you a future and a hope."[22] This future and the hope are not just for me; they are for my children and my children's children!

The arena calls us all, but you will pay a price. Getting into the arena is work. Getting into the arena takes time. Getting into the arena takes sacrifice and risk. At times, the battle seems hopeless. In the arena, our faith is tested and sharpened as fire does to steel. In the arena, courage and determined perseverance birth hope. In the arena, love and forgiveness will be found. In the arena, "the prayers of a righteous man availeth much."

Men, are you willing to climb into the arena to be a warrior for your children? They really have been waiting for you! "Fathers, do not provoke your children to anger, but bring them up in the discipline and instruction of the Lord" (Ephesians 6:4).

CHAPTER 8

ACTIONS VERSUS EMPTY WORDS

One of my shortcomings that I have perfected over years of working on the streets as a federal narcotics agent is that I have developed what I call the spiritual gift of criticism. After years of dealing with extremely dangerous and vile individuals, thieves, liars, and just plain evil human beings, I have a tendency to be very critical and cautious when dealing with others outside of my family and my profession. It is a rare occasion that I let my guard down outside of my home, including church and church functions.

During our assignment in Los Angeles, I invited a few of our closest friends (all narcotics agents) to church for Doug's baby dedication. The church had a very large congregation, and we were asked to come up on stage while the pastor prayed for and blessed the baby. We were in front of a throng of people, surrounded by close friends, and the pastor started introducing my family. He suddenly stopped and jokingly said, "Hey, by the way, don't mess with this group. They are all narcs. You better watch your step!"

As the congregation laughed, my best friend Steve whispered, "Is he trying to get us freaking killed?"

Following the prayer, we went back to our seats and spent the next thirty minutes looking over our shoulders as we swore we were being sized up for a hit at any moment. After the service, we left the church in a very hurried fashion. We were subsequently approached by what I immediately recognized as an unstable individual who demanded to talk to me. I quickly established a defensive posture, keeping the individual at arm's length. I gave him my business card and asked him to call me during the week. Although I never heard from the individual, I made a habit of sitting toward the back of the church throughout our remaining time in Los Angeles.

Growing up in that type of climate became normal and routine for our children. They began to get used to waiting for Dad to select where to sit in a restaurant, theater, or other venue. "We need the tactical advantage," I would often say, not realizing that I was conditioning them to become aware of their surroundings and potential external threats.

When we would go out for lunch or dinner when they were a little older—before I could say anything to the waiter or waitress who was seating us—Jessica or Doug would say, "Dad's not going to like this table." They were usually right. When we did find the right table, the kids would not sit down until I picked where I wanted to sit first. They became acutely aware when I would key on something happening and then witness me intervening in a situation in the street.

We were visiting Shelly's family in Pennsylvania one weekend when I decided to take the kids out to the movies. Shelly stayed with her sister, and I took four of my kids and a niece and nephew. I don't remember which Disney movie we saw, but the kids were all excited and talkative as we finished the movie and made our way back to the house.

A few miles from the house, a small car passed me at a high rate of speed—immediately followed by a police car. The patrol car put his emergency lights on and pulled behind the other vehicle, which began to pull to the side of the road. I slowed down and yelled for the kids to make sure they had their seat belts on. Jessica was watching what was transpiring from the back and yelled for to the kids to make sure they had their seatbelts on.

When the vehicles came to a stop the driver of the small car jumped out, slid across his hood, and ran into the woods with the police officer hot on his trail. Without much thought, I dropped the van into third gear and sped around the corner into an open field where I estimated the suspect and the police officer would come out. As the van skidded,

I hollered back to Jessica to make sure the doors were locked—and not to open anything unless a uniformed police officer came to the van.

Jessica told the kids to get down below the seats as I jumped out of the car, drawing my service revolver in pursuit of the suspect who had now eluded the officer. I eventually teamed up with a detective and assisted in searching the area for a brief time. After about twenty minutes with no results, I headed back to the van. Jessica was playing with the kids and keeping my niece and nephew calm. As I got into the van, Jess asked if I caught the bad guy. Upon hearing that I didn't, she commented that they would probably get him another day. I didn't think anything of the situation since it was the world and environment my children were growing up in—until I saw my nephew and niece. They looked absolutely traumatized by the entire event. As we returned to the house, I had to get somewhat creative in explaining to my sister-in-law that it was really nothing to be concerned about. I don't think they ever allowed their kids to ride with us again.

I expect that some readers are having a hard time understanding the climate I established and the world the kids grew up in. I did not teach them to think or act like everyone was a potential threat. Although this was the reality we lived in, I really did my best (hard as it was) to try to teach them to be balanced when dealing with individuals as a whole. I would often remind them to pray for wisdom when dealing with or sizing up other people. I taught them to treat people with dignity and respect and to always have compassion for those who were less fortunate.

Even though I had an extremely cautious and cynical persona due to my calling, I did realize that not everyone we encounter is liar, a thief, or a threat. Training the kids to understand the reality of living in an evil and corrupt world while being called to love and care for others was a challenging balancing act. I could talk about the importance of these issues until I was blue in the face, but it would be meaningless because teaching about our beliefs and values would be nothing more than hollow words if we failed to put them into action.

Not long after we moved to Virginia, it became necessary to buy a larger-capacity washing machine to keep up with the onslaught of daily laundry. Shelly placed an ad in the paper to sell the machine (that's what people did before Craigslist and eBay), and we soon received a response from an elderly couple. When they arrived, Shelly struck up a conversation and took an immediate liking to them both.

Shelly learned that they were in dire need of a washing machine, but they could not afford a new one. They had saved just enough money to buy the one we were offering. After a little more conversation, Shelly decided that we would just give them the machine. They were absolutely taken aback by her offer and accepted graciously. When they advised us that they would have to find someone to pick up and deliver the machine, Shelly told them we would be happy to do that for them since we had plenty of room in our van. The couple was extremely thankful and asked God to bless us and our family.

The older kids who had listened to the conversation were starting to get excited and giddy about what was happening. When the couple left, the kids barraged us with questions. Why are we giving it away? Don't they have enough money? Are they poor? Don't they have children who can help them?

Shelly's response was simple and to the point. She said, "Sometimes God places things on our hearts that He wants us to do and besides, kids, they need that washing machine much more than we need the money." Her response was met with nodding heads of the older ones, and the younger ones tried to make sense out of her statement.

We loaded up the washer and headed out toward the couple's double-wide trailer in rural northern Virginian. As we carried the machine into their home, the kids waited patiently in the van that was parked in the dirt driveway. As I hooked up the washer, Shelly learned that the couple had been going to a local coin-operated laundry since their washer and dryer were broken.

As we prepared to leave, we noticed the empty space where a dryer had once been. While heading out of the door, the elderly couple could not have thanked us or praised us more for the generosity we showed—and we delighted in long hugs and kind words.

Prior to leaving, Shelly looked over at me, and before she could say it, I blurted out that we were going to buy them a dryer. The kids immediately began to cheer and ask questions. We simply explained that they needed one. Two hours later, we arrived back at the couple's residence with a new dryer from Sears. They were extremely emotional and were at a loss for words except for constantly stating that we were an answer to prayer. On the way back to our house, the kids talked about the day's adventure and how the couple must have felt when we came back with a dryer.

Shelly and I didn't wake up every day and say, "What can we do today to teach the kids truth?" We simply tried to remember to utilize situations and opportunities to serve others as object lessons for our children. We were able to apply this experience to teach them the importance of understanding that there are times, more often than not, when it is necessary to consider others and their needs more important than our own. Furthermore, this situation allowed us to talk about how God utilized our family to answer the prayers of another family. That, as my older kids would say, is "pretty cool!"

Teaching the realities of a dangerous and corrupt world while being sensitive to the needs of others was a balancing act and sometimes led to actions that seemed contradictory to our teaching. For instance, I have always taught my children to be wary of strangers, not to get into cars of those they didn't know, and never to pick up a stranger in any situation. This day would be the exception to that rule.

We were on our way to church on a cold Virginia morning. The sun was shining, and there was still some snow and ice on the ground as we headed to church. As we made the usual turn on to the next road, we saw a very strange sight: an elderly woman bundled up in a heavy jacket, winter hat, and snow boots was hitchhiking. I slowed down as we passed her, looked at my wife, and said, "Are you kidding me!"

The older kids were shocked and pressed their faces against the window in disbelief. "Dad, why is she hitchhiking?"

I turned the van around and asked the woman if she was all right and if she needed a ride.

Without hesitation, she told me that she either missed her ride or they didn't show up. She was trying to get a ride to her church, which was in the opposite direction of where we were headed.

Shelly instructed the kids to open the sliding door to let her in. As we drove toward her church, she delighted in telling us about her life, her children, and her friends. As we passed an old cemetery, she pointed out the window and exclaimed, "Hey, kids, people are dying to get in there!" After which she chuckled to herself.

The kids looked on with amazement as the old woman continued to talk. When we arrived at her church, she thanked us, assured us she would be fine, and entered the building.

Driving away, we all were laughing. We were somewhat amazed at what we had just gone through—and how at ease the old woman had been. One of the kids asked if we were still going to church. I thought for a second and then replied, "I think we just went to church, right?" I glanced back in the rear-view mirror to see the puzzled looks of some of the kids. I went on to tell them that we go to church to hear about God's love, to learn what He did for us, and to see how we should act and treat others.

I saw some nodding heads and asked if they would agree that this morning it was more important to help an elderly woman get to her church than to pass her by and go to our church.

They all yelled and screamed, "Yes."

"Great," I said. "So, today we actually demonstrated what we are learning at church, right?"

"Right," they all yelled.

As we pulled into our driveway, I looked back and said, "One more thing. Never, ever, ever pick up a hitchhiker or a stranger, do you understand?"

They all smiled and said yes.

I would subsequently have the opportunity to discuss with the older kids what the difference in this situation (given my profession) and being presented with the same situation if they were alone—balance, balance, balance!

Throughout my career, I along with tens of thousands of other warriors and public servants have witnessed human suffering and tragedy up close and sometimes on a grand scale. We like to tell others outside of our calling and profession that you get numb to it. In reality, most of our hearts still break when confronted with the suffering of others. I have often reminded men and women in my profession—and outside of my profession—to never lose compassion for another human being. Never let your experiences scar your conscience so deeply that you lose your ability to care about others you come into contact with on a daily basis.

Compassion literally means "to suffer together." Among emotion researchers, it is defined as the feeling that arises when you are confronted with another's suffering and feel motivated to relieve that suffering.[23] There are, however, a number of individuals who are solely responsible for the cause of their suffering. As such, true compassion forces us to push aside things we know are true in order to assist someone in need.

As we were stationed in a number of cities, the kids would often see homeless individuals on street corners, under highway overpasses, or walking down the street. I explained that there were a number of individuals who were "panhandlers" and were pretending to be homeless in order to have people give them money as a way of making a living. I explained that there were thousands of people who actually were homeless and lived on the street due to a number of reasons. The majority of homeless individuals I came into contact with suffered from a host of mental health issues, including drug and alcohol addiction. Some of these individuals were extremely dangerous due to their psychosis and/or addictions. They often preferred to live on the street than to go to a shelter, which was hard for the children to understand. I would tell them not to stop and give money to people on the street corner because they would simply use it to buy drugs and/or alcohol, which ultimately would aggravate their already deteriorated condition.

Several years ago, we were heading into Dallas to attend a Christmas performance at one of the downtown theaters. As we pulled onto the frontage road, we saw a homeless man, covered in dirt from head to toe, with his hand held out. As we crept closer toward the intersection, I could see the desperation on his face and in his demeanor. All I could think about, especially given the holiday season, was that he was someone's son—maybe even someone's father, brother, family member.

I was overcome with thoughts about how he came to be here, even though I was fully aware of the probability of his journey. As we came alongside of him, I stopped the car, asked my wife for money, and handed the man a twenty-dollar bill. He very quietly muttered a thank you and walked back toward the overpass where he was likely living.

Most of my children in the car at the time were much older and remained quiet as we drove away.

One of my sons asked, "Hey, Dad, don't you think he will use that for booze or drugs?"

I paused briefly and said, "Son, I don't know if he will use it to buy drugs or booze, and quite honestly, I realized some time ago that I was wrong about how I felt about many people in that situation. It's not up to me to decide what they will or won't do with any money I give. What I do know right now is what I saw on his face, and if a bottle or a drug gets him to survive through the day or night, then so be it. I can't heal the man. I can't change him. That has to be left up to the Lord at this moment. What I can do is simply be a little compassionate by giving him some cash to help alleviate a few of his circumstances right now."

We talked a little more about the importance of never losing compassion for others and how our perceptions about someone else's circumstances can be false or wrong.

Teaching the realities of a dangerous and corrupt world while being sensitive to the needs of others was a balancing act that sometimes led to actions that were contradictory to our earlier teachings. However, during these moments, Shelly and I were able to recognize that the children were growing and learning and that we were also maturing and growing in our faith. We realized it was important for them to understand where we had been wrong about certain issues and why we were wrong. That often led to great discussions about constantly being open and always being willing to learn and grow in wisdom, knowledge, and faith.

CHAPTER 9

DATING, DRUGS, AND THE INTERNET

I talked earlier about discussing sex with the children at a certain point in their lives, but that was more of an introduction of what sex is and how babies were created. As each of them matured and began to enter the dating arena, we would often discuss the importance of individual honor, which is having a high regard for themselves as well as the person they were dating. There were times we would talk about the battle going on in our minds—and how personal desires and emotions had the ability to take you to a place you didn't intend to go.

All of us struggle with wanting to satisfy our personal, selfish desires over what is honorable, healthy, and respectful rather than sacrificing now for the prize at the end. The battleground, we would explain, is in your head as we continually struggle with our desires and wants over our needs. Again, we would remind them that the Lord designed us to be attracted to one another and that sex was more than an act of pleasure. It was a physical, emotional, and spiritual connection between a man and a woman, intended to be performed within the bounds of marriage.

We would explain (at the appropriate time) that one of the greatest gifts you can give your wife or husband is yourself and that romantic love and intimacy in a marriage relationship was established by God. "For this reason a man will leave his father and mother and be united to his wife, and the two will become one flesh."[24] While we hoped and prayed they would not have to deal with the regrets of youthful indiscretions, we fully recognized that ultimately it would be their decision to make and bring to bear. That is why we never said that horrific things would happen to them if they made mistakes or bad judgments. We explained that we were designed by a loving God who understands our humanity and our fallibility. He is quick to forgive us when we fall, and He is willing and able to reach down, pick us up, dust us off, and encourage us to get back into the arena.

There really was not a lot of dating for any of my kids during high school as I remember. However, any introduction of a so-called boyfriend or girlfriend was a spectacle and a fire walk in our home. I was—and still am—the kind of dad who young men fear the most, and I honestly believe that fear is a great tool if wielded wisely.

During the high school years, I made it a habit to simply ignore the existence of any young man visiting one of my daughters. Shelly would often introduce me, which was routinely followed by a simple nod and a look of derision on my part. I called them "sniffers." In my mind, they were sniffing around and looking for something to take, steal, and covet. I would not give them the opportunity to think they were liked or approved of by me. It didn't matter to me if they went to our church, attended Bible study, or hoped to be a pastor someday— they were simply sniffers!

Regardless of their backgrounds, there were absolute rules when they came to the house. You absolutely don't go into my daughter's bedroom. I don't care if you leave the door open, you don't go in to that sacred place! I would ask a list of questions and find out where he lived, what his dad and mother did, who he hung out with, what he believed, and on and on and on.

My kids would often ask, "Why all the questions? Why does that matter?"

I would simply say, "Because I love you so much that if something happens to you or you suddenly become missing, I need to be able to identify who I am going to go after and hurt in order to find you or find out what happened!" As hard as this might be, I want the reader to understand that this was not simply dad bravado. I am not the dad who cleans his gun in the presence of a boyfriend in order to scare and intimidate. In my mind, I am the dad who is capable of making Liam Neeson's character in *Taken* a lightweight if needed—and the young "sniffers" who came around understood that.

On a Saturday morning while we were stationed in Virginia, my oldest daughter came up to me and said, "Dad, I already told Mom this, and she said it was okay. My friend (a boy) is coming to pick me up this afternoon. He is coming with his friend in a truck, and we are going to go out for something to eat."

I immediately responded by asking her what the friend's name was, where he lived, what kind of truck he had.

My daughter replied that she did not know.

"Well, I guess I will find out when they get here."

She begged me not to. She nervously paced in the foyer, looking out the panel windows for her ride to show up when she suddenly yelled good-bye and headed out the front door. She didn't realize that I was on her heels as she jumped into the back of a beautiful, new dually pickup truck.

As I held open the passenger door, I noticed a total of three young boys in the truck. I pointed to the driver and asked, "Who are you and where do you live?

He immediately responded. I looked at the young man in the passenger seat and asked him the same thing, and he responded that he was being dropped off up the street.

In the back, my daughter was sitting quietly next to her friend (a boy). I pointed to my daughter and said, "Do you all see this young woman? This is my daughter. While she is in this truck or anywhere out with you, you are to consider her precious cargo that has to be treated with the utmost respect. She will not come back to this house with a scratch, bruise, or blemish. Do you understand?"

At that all three emphatically replied, "Yes, sir!"

"Okay. Have a nice day," I said and walked inside the house.

I didn't think anything of the incident until a few days later.

While getting ready for bed one evening, Shelly said that my daughter told her how I scared the living hell out of the boys in the pickup truck the other day.

I muttered, "Good."

My daughter told her how scared the boys were of me and how they couldn't believe I asked them questions and then pointed out how important it was to make sure she was treated and cared for. The boys kept asking her why her dad did that. Shelly paused for a moment, looked at me, and asked if I wanted to know what her answer was. I expected that it was something along the lines that her dad didn't like boys or didn't trust anyone, but that wasn't even close to her response. My daughter responded to the boys' questions by simply stating, "My daddy loves me. That's why." This was incredibly powerful for me to hear. Although I was somewhat of a brute to her friends, she recognized that I had her interests and her interests alone as my priority because I love her and want my children to succeed and thrive in life.

In order for them to succeed and thrive, we had to be willing to have a dialogue with the kids on every issue—regardless of the subject matter. Again, this is never about trying to develop so-called perfect little Christian men and women. It was about preparing them for the trials and challenges of a corrupt culture that would gladly walk them down a path that leads right to quicksand and/or destruction.

Although establishing a foundation of faith based upon our Christian beliefs was critical, we also looked at parenting as establishing a series of road signs to follow in order to do our best to instruct them how to avoid quicksand or crashing. For instance, think of the types of signs that require us to utilize caution on the road; sharp curve ahead, do not enter, one way, steep grade, beware of falling rocks, or don't feed the bears. You may not find that one on the road, but you get where I am going on this. Road signs are displayed to warn us about danger ahead or to direct us about how to avoid an accident. When we consistently follow the road signs, we develop driving habits that subsequently minimize the danger of being out on the highway as a driver. However, we still need to learn how to drive defensively because other drivers who refuse to heed the same road signs can and will become a danger to you out on the road if you are not attentive.

In the same way, we have to be mindful of who we decide to take in our car as a passenger since they might encourage us to disregard the warning signs ahead.

Some people have actually told me that the reason our kids have done well is because I was in federal law enforcement. I always respond with a hearty laugh. I have known dozens of law enforcement professionals who have children who are dealing with emotional issues as well as substance abuse on a variety of levels. Why Johnny or Susie decides to experiment with drugs is a result of a number of factors, including simply making the wrong choice. We have always recognized that our children are quite capable of the most heinous activity because of the sin nature of humanity. We could do everything right, and they are still capable of making the absolute wrong decision that lead to a life of suffering and abuse. We have done our best to hold up the warning signs of making those harmful decisions, and by the good Lord's grace, they have all decided to avoid the drug culture.

We also talked to our children about drug use and abuse very openly. In particular, I spent a great deal of time talking to them about the dangers of marijuana due to the false narrative consistently touted in the media that the drug is a medicine and is harmless. Having served close to three decades as a narcotics agent, I can state emphatically as a witness to the consequences of its use and abuse, marijuana is a dangerous drug, and it is—and has been—a gateway drug. Unfortunately, for the past thirty years, the marijuana legalization movement has aggressively promoted and bemoaned that the war on drugs is lost and the US is doing nothing but locking up addicts and users. This rhetoric spewed by legalizers, libertarians, talking media heads, and many in congress is a tactic utilizing emotional capital combined with fallacious information about the horrors of the drug war to seek drug legalization under the guise of liberty, capitalism, and countering racial bias.

Those of us who have challenged the assertions made by these groups with actual facts that prove otherwise have routinely been attacked professionally and personally, alleging nefarious motives for our positions. I have often found these responses laughable and sad. These supposedly reasonable and intelligent people are hell-bent on the destruction of the next generation of Americans. Marijuana legalization targets the most vulnerable in our society: our children. Regardless of what is touted by the media, not everyone in the country has tried marijuana. We know that not everyone who tries marijuana will become addicted or move on to other drugs, but one out of eight children will.

The reality we face as parents and citizens is that as legalization of marijuana becomes more popular—based on misinformation, outright lies, and false studies—it will not stop at marijuana. There is currently a groundswell being pushed for the legalization of small amounts of all drugs regardless of their respective dangers. The price of this ludicrous and irresponsible positioning will be paid by parents and citizens as we continue to lose generations of children to substance abuse. Once something is legal, it is considered morally acceptable. We lose nearly forty thousand people per year to substance abuse. How morally acceptable is that for us?

The economic cost to the American society due to substance abuse and addiction now exceeds $600 billion annually. These figures include tobacco, alcohol, and illicit substances. To suggest that legalizing any illicit drug will have a positive impact on this number or the safety and security of our society is illogical. In fact, legalizing marijuana or any other illicit substance will do nothing but increase users and increase the societal costs burdened by our country. Time and time again, researchers, social scientists, and law enforcement professionals have witnessed that, as the perception of harm for marijuana or any drug decreases, there is a corresponding increase in use and abuse.

I challenge the reader to take a critical look at the acute issues arising in Colorado and Washington since passing recreational marijuana legislation. On a recent trip to Denver, my youngest son sent a text to his brothers and sisters describing the city as reminding him of "Gotham City" from the Batman movies. He described the city as containing scores of homeless kids, fights, dirty streets, and panhandlers on every corner.

Regulations and regulatory processes and procedures are often touted as the answer to mitigate use and abuse of a proposed legalized substance. I have been told a number of times that it is easier for kids to get marijuana than alcohol because, as they say, alcohol is regulated. During an event I attended some years ago, I challenged a former school administrator for making that statement and asked him what his factual basis was. His reply was to ask any school kid. The fact is that marijuana use by teens is second to the use of alcohol by teens in almost every state. So much for the regulatory process having a mitigating effect on use and abuse! There is growing evidence that more young people are seeking treatment for marijuana dependence than all the other illicit drugs combined. This figure alone should cause us to think critically about the consequences of pursuing outright legalization in the United States.

During my testimony before the Senate Drug Caucus more than two years ago, I made the statement that drug legalization in our country is reckless and irresponsible for reasons that I articulated as well as from my years of experience as a federal narcotics agent. During my tenure as a government executive, I routinely advised legislators, civic leaders, and members of the Department of Justice that we have a responsibility to the next generation. If we disregard the drug issue in our country under the guise of liberty, we must be willing to accept the consequences that are sure to come.

Following my testimony, I received a copy of a letter that was sent to President Obama. It was signed by several members of Congress— from both sides of the aisle—and declared my statement before the senate "served no purpose other than to inflame passions and misinform the public."[25] I was taken aback by how callous disregard for the truth based on evidence could be dismissed by those who are sworn to uphold the Constitution and ensure that the next generation has an opportunity to be successful.

Those legislators forgot that the first duty of government is the protection and security of the governed—even if that means protecting them from harming themselves. I would again ask, "Does the truth matter?" I find it terribly ironic that if you spend any amount of time in Denver or the surrounding cities, you will find an explosion of advertising signs imploring parents to talk to their children about drug use. The parent talk is suddenly important to Colorado legislators largely because Colorado drug use among teens is now higher than the national average.

We can no longer expect our legislators to have the safety and security of our children as a priority when it comes to drug legalization or any other number of issues impacting our children. I know this may sound harsh and conspiratorial, but consider the number of millionaires and billionaires who donate vast sums of money into the legalization movement. Why would global businessmen and businesswomen want to influence legislation to ensure that we produce a pharmaceutically induced young population who are disengaged from the body politic and/or their duties as citizens? One of my favorite books of all time is *How Do You Kill 11 Million People* by Andy Andrews. In this very short book Andy asks how it was possible for the Nazi regime during World War II to kill eleven million of their own people with little to no resistance. He posits that the "answer is breathtakingly simple and still being used by some elected leaders to achieve various goals today … Lie to them."[26]

The topic of drug use and experimentation was discussed with a relative amount of reasoning and logic. We tried our best to avoid telling the kids that the reason not to make poor choices regarding drug use was that we, as parents, would be angry. Rather, we would offer up the visual image of a bunch of their friends swimming in a septic tank filled with sewage and encouraging them to jump in because the water is great. You can see that it is filthy. You can smell that it is bad. Are you willing to listen to their obvious lies in order to fit in and avoid the truth? The road signs are everywhere. They just have to be willing to seek the truth in order to avoid the dangerous traps, and some of those traps are uniquely insidious, snaring a willing subject with just one push of a button.

The advancement of technology in our culture has certainly afforded us the opportunity to get answers with one click of a button. In an instant, we can live-stream video from space probes orbiting Jupiter or watch the birth of a bald eagle high atop a mountainous cliff in a remote region of the world. Buying a local newspaper or book is becoming obsolete since it has become easier to download information rather than to drive to the bookstore.

I recently read (online) how online shopping is at an all-time high and how some grocery chains are exploring how to exploit the same type of services. Businesses across the landscape are making it easier and easier for consumers to never leave their homes by shopping with just one click of a button. Yet that same click has the ability to take them to online sites that have the ability to harm and corrupt young and older minds alike. Gone are the days when young boys would sneak a look at a *Playboy* magazine to view pictures of naked women in erotic poses. Now one click will afford anyone to anonymously visit a multitude of sites—day or night—where they can view any and all types of graphic sex videos, buy illicit drugs, or find any number of harmful substances. The Internet, while an amazing tool and resource for many, is also a convenient path that has the potential to corrupt young minds. It presents unique challenges for families today.

Our first family computer was located in my office on the first floor of our home in Virginia. We actually took time to explain to the kids what a great tool it was, but we told them that they had to be careful when utilizing a search engine. Any small mistake could take them to a site that they had no intention of viewing. We had warned them to stay out of chat rooms, which were popular at the time, because of the likelihood of predators hiding anonymously behind the Internet. We constantly reminded them to call us right away if something bad came up on the screen.

One evening, one of my younger daughters screamed for Shelly and me to come to the office. As we entered the office, we could see my daughter hiding her face with one hand and pointing to the screen with another. She had inadvertently typed in the wrong name of a person, and one click later, up came the naked pictures of a man and woman on a pornographic web site. Because of her age, she couldn't fully understand why such sites existed. However, it afforded us the opportunity to discuss the situation with all of them and explain how these sites could be traps for young minds.

Months later, I was researching a project online when I hit the back button a number of times to get to a previous screen. In seconds, a site identified as celebrity sex photos came up on the screen with a host of naked females in a pictorial. I realized that one of the kids must have visited the site, and I called for Shelly to come in. As she came around the desk, she took one look at the screen—and looked at me as though I was the guilty party.

When I explained to her what I had done and that I thought one of the kids had visited the site, she instructed me to go to the history tab to review all the sites visited. It didn't take much detective work to find out what the history showed: Pokémon, Pokémon, SpongeBob, celebrity sex photos, no cold trail here.

Shelly asked how I wanted to handle the situation.

At first, I struggled with the answer. I knew which son was on the computer, but I did not want to embarrass him further by making him feel like he was some type of deviant. I shot from the hip and called him into the office. As I began to tell him what happened, I could see the embarrassment growing on his face. I asked him if he visited the site, and he sheepishly admitted to it. I then asked the dumbest question I could have asked: "Why?" Seriously, I knew why he visited the site, for the same reason why I probably stayed a little too long on that same site trying to "figure out" who was the culprit!

He didn't have an answer to my dumb question, but it gave us an opportunity to talk about how men are designed to be attracted to women. I explained how that attraction can be perverted by allowing unrealistic pictures to become embedded in our brains, which is more powerful and can hold more information than any computer. I told him, "garbage in, garbage out." We discussed how the greatest battles we face are in our minds and how we are constantly pulled towards selfish desires; the flesh is constantly at war with the spirit. It was a good talk, and he left without thinking that his mom or dad thought any less of him. Although we had some limited filters on our computer, the situation made it very clear to us that we had not done enough to keep our children out of the trappings of these sites. We had to reconfigure the computer so none of those sites were accessible.

Teaching the truth about a host of issues can be uncomfortable for parents and for children. However, understanding that the truth matters and that we can know and teach truth to our children was and still is critical to healthy growth. At the same time, we never minimized the fact that speaking truth to power takes courage, commitment, and passion—and is sometimes met with unwarranted consequences to the truth bearer.

CHAPTER 10

LEARNING TO TRUST GOD

In almost every speaking presentation I give, I routinely start out by telling the audience that I love my life. I absolutely love my life. I am a very ordinary, fallible man who has led an outstanding, extraordinary life, and I want them to know that I continually thank God almost every day for blessing me with the things I really needed rather than the things I wanted. I never say my life is perfect. I never say that I don't have wounds. I don't say that I have never faced adversity, tragedy, or difficult seasons. I simply tell them that I love my life—warts, bruises, mistakes, and all! It has been said that adversity builds character, and while that may be true for some, we believe and can testify that adversity really exposes your character while challenging and strengthening your faith.

As far back as I can remember, we consistently taught the kids that we worship a loving God who willingly invades the lives of those who make a conscious decision to accept Him. While that same God operates in the affairs of His people in a great way, there are things that may happen in our lives that we are unable to understand. Shelly and I would explain that bad things sometimes happen to good people. Friends and family members get sick and die. Life sometimes is not fair, yet that does not disqualify the Lord from being God—or us from believing that when we cry out to Him, He will answer. Faith requires us to trust Him as He is the One that holds all things together. Yet there are times that trust is severely tested when things go wrong in our lives.

I was just about to leave for court in Los Angeles when Shelly called to let me know that she was picking up Jessica from school because her knee still hurt from a fall a few days earlier. Shelly had made an appointment with our pediatrician and would be going directly to the doctor's office.

Several hours later, I was still at the courthouse when I received a 911 page (no cell phones yet) from Shelly. It was very unusual to receive that kind of page, but I was sure that it had to do with Jessica and her knee. Prior to exiting the courthouse, I received another page with several 911 digits followed by the clinic phone number. I jumped on the pay phone outside the courthouse and called the number.

Shelly tried her best to explain the situation. "Micah ... not breathing ... turned blue ... not good ... please get here!" Micah had been born just two weeks earlier via C-section but with no complications. While the doctor was seeing Jessica, Micah's face began turning blue. She summoned the doctor who immediately ripped off Micah's clothes while asking how long he had been like that. Shelly had no idea. She had just noticed that he seemed to be struggling. He was a born very healthy, and as far as we knew, there were no medical issues.

With lights and sirens blasting, I raced all the way to the clinic's door. The clinic was empty except for my kids who were all being watched by a close friend in the waiting room. In the treatment room, my heart sank when I saw the doctor holding an oxygen mask over the mouth and nose of a fragile grayish-blue infant. Micah was struggling for every breath, and his tiny chest seemed to collapse on itself as he fought to breathe. Shelly was standing next to them with an unrecognizable expression. She was almost blank with disbelief. I had seen the faces of critically ill and dying babies during my years as a pediatric corpsman in the navy, but this time, it was my son.

I would like to be able to say that my Christian faith caused me to immediately call out to God and ask him to heal Micah, but I thought, *Lord, you are going to take him away from me, aren't you?*

Faced with the unknown, the agony and fear of losing a child began to push my faith out of the way. I couldn't find the words to pray at all. As the ambulance crew arrived, the last thing my wife heard as she entered the back of the ambulance was the pediatrician saying, "You need to get this child to the hospital fast. He is not going to make it!"

When I arrived at the hospital, Shelly was waiting on the pediatric floor while a pediatric pulmonary specialist examined Micah. We waited very nervously until the doctor came and spoke with us.

The doctor stood in front of us, placed his hand on Shelly's shoulder, and smiled. "Mom and Dad, your child is going to be fine. He has a pneumonia that probably has been developing since shortly after his birth. The worst thing that may happen is that we may have to perform a tracheotomy—but only if he doesn't improve in a few days. We are lucky that we caught this early since it could have progressed very seriously in a short amount of time."

We were relieved about the diagnosis, but we were still worried about his prognosis. That evening, we received a surprise visit from our assistant pastor and another member of our church. They took the time to pray with us for strength and comfort and spent time praying over Micah for healing and health. The following morning, the doctor advised us that Micah's condition had improved exponentially overnight. Based on his remarkable improvement, he would not require a tracheotomy, but he would remain in the hospital for the next week for treatment and observation.

Following his release from the hospital, we marveled and thanked God for the sequence of events that led up to him being treated. We told Jessica that she actually saved Micah's life because she went to the doctor's office initially. Had we not gone, it is likely that Shelly would have put Micah in his crib where he would have died from lack of oxygen.

We talked with the kids about how it was an example of the Lord moving in our lives and answering prayer, but there is more to the story. It still brings me to tears when I consider how God answers his children before we even ask Him to move. Jessica told us that her knee really didn't hurt that badly, but she had an overwhelming sense that she needed to call her mom. The school nurse looked at her knee and wanted Jessica to go back to class, but Jessica—very uncharacteristically—demanded that she be able to call her mom at home. She would not take no for an answer. When she contacted Shelly, she said she needed to leave school because her knee hurt, which caused Shelly to get the appointment.

When we pushed her on why she had to call Shelly, Jessica could only say was that she just was driven by something deep inside her. We explained that it was the spirit of the living God. He chose that instance to use her to save Micah's life. We explained that instances such as that tend to galvanize our faith and trust in God, but when unexplained tragic events occur, faith and trust are tested. It causes us to be shaken while finding the courage to trust the Lord even in the darkest times.

It was unusual for my oldest brother to call so early on the morning of April 9, 2008. I answered the call with an upbeat hello, only to hear back the broken voice of my brother say, "They got him. The notification team just left. They got Tony Jr."

The reality of war had come knocking on our family's door with vicious ferocity. My nephew, Tech Sergeant Anthony L. Capra was an explosive ordinance technician in the US Air Force. On the morning of April 9, 2008, supported by a Special Forces team, Tony Jr. defused a massive IED in Golden Hills, Iraq. Tony Jr. didn't know that the bomb was tied to another device, which was a booby trap. In an instant, Tony Jr.—a son, a brother, and a husband, the father of five, the oldest of twelve children, and a devout Christian—was gone.

I fell to my knees by the side of my desk as my brother told me he had to get to Tony Jr.'s family in Maryland. As I drove home, I called Shelly at work and told her to contact the older kids who were away at college. I remember my conversation with God all the way home. I asked why over and over again. It didn't make sense. How could He let this happen?

In the midst of our collective sorrow, my brother, a retired air force lieutenant colonel declared we needed to "circle the wagons, lean on each other, and lean on our faith." We did just that throughout the days and weeks leading up to his burial in Arlington National Cemetery.

During the funeral service, Tony Jr.'s brother, a US Air Force physician, told us all that Tony lived in victory each day of his life. He made a positive difference for everyone he came in contact with. On that fateful morning, because of his heroic and selfless actions, untold numbers of soldiers and civilians would be spared death or injury. Still, all the memorials, speeches, and ceremonies could not diminish the loss that his family is left to bear. Even now, we realize that time does not heal all wounds. Our faith and fond memories help us live with the pain of loss and the knowledge that we will see him again.

In the midst of grief and sorrow, well-meaning people—even within our Christian community—say stupid things, thinking it will comfort those who are grieving. Unfortunately, telling someone of faith that it was God's will for his or her child to die is incredibly ignorant on a number of levels. I often advise my family and those who ask that the best thing we can do for someone who is grieving the loss of a loved one is to love them, hug them, cry with them, and pray for the Lord's peace and comfort for them. Don't try to justify or explain their loss during their most vulnerable emotional season. Consider that even Jesus wept when told that Lazarus had died—even though He knew He was going to raise Lazarus from the dead.[27] Jesus had compassion for those who were grieving and dealing with the burden of loss even though He knew it was temporary.

Shelly and I attempted to teach the children the same thing when it came to grief and sorrow: it is a temporary condition here on earth because those of us with a relationship with Christ will see each other again as promised in the Bible. "But we do not want you to be ignorant, brothers, about those who have died, so that you may not grieve like other people who have no hope."[28]

Even in grief, we have a confident expectation that we will see our loved ones again as promised, and this is precisely where we cling to our faith and trust as believers. Still we had to deal with the questions of "why" and "if God loves us, why did He let that bad thing happen?" In dealing with the loss of my nephew, I remember explaining that I was pretty confident that God didn't just decide to take Tony from us like moving a chess piece during a game. Although we live in a fallen world where bad things happen to good people, we must rely on the promise that God works for the good of those who love him. The kids seemed to understand this position and answer, but I knew it did not really answer a skeptic who might say that our God must not care about us or that He is a cosmic bully—until I started to better understand love and free will.

In the book of Matthew, Jesus was asked what was the greatest commandment. He answered, "'Love the Lord your God with all your heart and with all your soul and with all your mind. This is the first and greatest commandment. And the second is like it: 'Love your neighbor as yourself.' All the Law and the Prophets hang on these two commandments." [29]

Love is the supreme ethic for humanity given to us by God.[30] Therefore, love is a conscious act of the will, and in order for a person to truly love someone, he or she must have freedom of the will. Even though God says that the love of God is the greatest command, He has given us the free will to choose for ourselves to follow that command. If He were to simply force us to love, if that were possible, we would simply be complying with the command and not choosing for ourselves to follow it. That violates our free will—and then it would be appropriate to call Him a cosmic bully.

By the same token, asking God to intercede in the free will of men in order to stop so-called bad things from happening would be like asking God to take away our free will. We would simply become cosmic robots without the freedom to choose right and wrong. God's love for us is so unfathomable that He simply asks us to choose Him and His ways. When we refuse, He respects our choice. Tragic and heinous things happen largely due to man's free will, and recognizing this should cause us as believers to trust God's supreme wisdom and knowledge that He is a just God. While he may not interfere with our free will, we can be assured that He will "work all things for good for those who love him."[31]

Dr. Ravi Zacharias said, "Sometimes when we see the heinousness of evil, we may also witness the majesty, love and goodness of God."[32]

Discussing death in our house was not necessarily a regular topic around the dinner table, but we never avoided talking about it with the kids. As a matter of fact, we would often remind the kids that we are not promised tomorrow—or even tonight—and that our faith instructs us that we have no reason to fear death.

A number of years ago, Shelly and I were preparing to travel together when I realized that if something happened to us both, the kids had no instructions about how to proceed with the house and finances. Although our life insurance and other financial paperwork was in order, I decided to write a one-page letter to my oldest daughter with instructions for what to do with the house, how to care for her siblings' education, and who to immediately contact to assist them. The letter became comically known as the "death note" in our family. To this day, anytime Shelly and I travel together, especially by airplane, I remind one of the kids where to find the letter. The response is always the same: "I know, Dad. The instructions are in the death note!"

As I have told them on numerous occasions, we are always in training for the next season—even if that next season is departing from this life. We have a responsibility to be prepared for that journey. When I was a child, my father taught us that death was not to be feared. It was like taking off your shoe. Your shoe (the body) was just a covering, and when you shed it, you were able to get to your new location, your real home, which was heaven.

We had the distinct pleasure as a family of having my mother live with us during the last five years of her life. My mom was, without a doubt, the single reason why her children have succeeded in life. She devoted her life to praying for us and was the living embodiment of what it meant to trust God in everything. Even when dealing with her grandson's death, she would often declare that God held our tears in His hands and that He would eventually make something great come from our loss. My kids referred to her as "G," which was short for Grandma. In the last few years of her life, she would often tell our kids how she was ready to die. She was tired of being ill and missed her husband, who had been gone for over twenty years. My kids, especially the girls, would get mad at her and tell her not to say that "because God must want you to still be here for a reason."

Mom was rushed to the hospital one morning following a heart attack. After she was stabilized, I entered her room and held her hand. She looked at me and spoke to me through her oxygen mask. She made me promise not to do anything to bring her back if she died. "I am ready to go, and I want to see my husband," she said with confidence and not a shred of fear.

"I promise, Mom," I said.

The kids initially didn't understand why G felt that way, and all I could tell them was that she was absolutely ready to leave this world—and she was now looking forward to spending eternity with God and the loved ones who had preceded her.

As I held her hand one morning, I saw the heart monitor begin to fluctuate. Holding back tears, I leaned toward her and whispered, "Mom, I think it's time for you to go home."

The nurses walked in immediately and said that she was gone.

Shelly arrived only seconds after her passing, saw Mom's body from the doorway, and said, "She's gone home already!"

Mom knew what it took and what it meant to love and trust the unseen hand of God. She was a great role model for me as well as my children for how we should live a life of faith. It was my honor as her son to watch as Mom left the shoe behind as Dad had taught. She was on her way to her new home.

CHAPTER 11

DEALING WITH FAILURE AND ADVERSITY

I have had the honor of serving in three military services and have nearly three decades as a federal narcotics agent. In every training academy I have attended, there is an increasing amount of mental stress, physical stress, and repetitive training as each week and month goes by. Military and police instructors and trainers push recruits sometimes to the brink of their respective abilities in order to prepare them physically, mentally, and psychologically for combat. They do this because actual combat, whether in the jungles or deserts in a foreign land or on the city streets in the United States, is exponentially worse.

During my profession, I learned to "train the way we fight and fight the way we train." An essential part of my training was learning that just because you are wounded, you must stay in the fight. You must do everything you can to fight through the pain—mentally and aggressively—and never give up. In numerous training scenarios, I would hear instructors repeatedly remind students that getting wounded does not mean you will die. You must push through to fight and live. Some of this training came as a result of a study several decades ago regarding police officers wounded in the line of duty. The study identified a number of officers who received non-life-threatening wounds, disengaged from the fight, and literally went into shock and died. The study concluded that these officers were psychologically conditioned due to any number of reasons to believe that if they were wounded, they were likely to die. Therefore, they were out of the fight. The same is true with life. If you have never been in a fight, if you have never had any adversity in your life, if you have never prepared yourself what to do after getting punched in the face, there is a good likelihood that you will stay down when you get punched.

Over the years, Shelly and I have witnessed some of the most psychologically damaging things done to young children by adults under the guise of protecting their self-esteem. These things include not keeping score at athletic events, saying everyone is a winner, giving everyone a trophy, and claiming that we are all equal in terms of athletic and/or academic ability. We are so busy protecting their self-esteem that we don't see the harm we are doing early in their lives by not preparing them for the punch in the face that absolutely will come! This is not only done in the academic environment; we are witnessing more and more parents being overprotective and shielding their children from any and all adversity.

Helicopter parenting refers to a style of parenting that is overprotective and takes too much responsibility for children's experiences, successes, and failures, leading to over-controlling, overprotecting, and over-perfecting.[33] In an effort to shield children from adversity, failure, and the unfairness of life, some parents are raising weak-minded snowflakes that will easily crumple to the floor as soon as they are introduced to any adversity that comes their way. This is precisely why young college students today are demanding safe places where words can't hurt them. They have been conditioned to be offended by words, looks, beliefs, positions, and opinions, especially when the metaphoric punch comes.

All of our children played sports in high school, and we encouraged them all to attempt to compete in at least two different sporting events during the school year—and most of them did. They were all relatively good athletes and played softball, football, wrestling, volleyball, or field hockey. Competing in sporting events provided great teaching opportunities in life. While we encouraged them to do their best and excel at whatever sport they were involved in—no matter how hard they practiced or how well they played—sometimes they lost because the other team or opponent was better. We would often tell them that they could do everything right in sports and in life and still fail in their pursuits. Just because you fail at something doesn't mean you are out of the game. It doesn't mean you are out of the fight. It doesn't mean your life is over or has no meaning.

It is not failure that will keep you down—it is how you react to failure that will impact your future. There is a cost one must pay in order to win or be successful in any endeavor because there is no real success without some type of personal sacrifice. That cost is a willingness to work hard, study hard, learn from trials and failures, and push through physical or emotional pain. Adversity and failure are a part of life, and as parents, it was necessary to watch our children stumble and fail sometimes in order for them to understand the cost of obtaining success.

When they stumbled or failed, we would at times hold out our hands to pull them up, dust them off, and encourage them to get back into the arena to fight for the things they wanted to pursue. We refrained from coddling them or shielding them from any type of trial or pain. Adversity doesn't build character. It exposes character. We prayed that, when they found themselves in the midst of the proving grounds of life, they would lean heavily on their personal beliefs and training, which would ultimately flesh out in how they reacted to adversity or failure.

We understood that suffering through failure and adversity provided great opportunities for Shelly and me to motivate them to improve, succeed, and move beyond the loss or failure and pursue excellence. I would often tell them to never stop fighting and to never give up. The only time you stop is when you are dead. I know this sounds somewhat dark, but we knew it was important to have them mentally prepared for when they moved out of our house and from our protection and were out on their own. While we did our best to prepare them for the battles ahead, they were always advised that if they found themselves in quicksand—with no way out or no escape— home would be a temporary refuge if needed.

Our oldest daughter decided to attend a university in the Northeast to study meteorology. I would often tell Jessica that I could see her on television, discussing the highs and lows of the weather in the region and how great she would be as a meteorologist. We took the drive from Fredericksburg, Virginia, to Danbury, Connecticut, to drop her off for her freshman fall semester. After setting up her dorm room with all the college necessities, we gathered in front of her dorm to say good-bye. My two younger daughters were crying quite hard as they hung on to Jessica, not wanting to let her go.

As we pulled them away to place them in the car, Jessica looked at me crying and said quietly, "Daddy, I don't want to go to college." In an instant, the reality that she was breaking away from Mom, Dad, and her family suddenly became evident to her. The moment that she couldn't wait for—the moment she dreamed about and was more than anxious to pursue—was now met with some concern and a little fear. What made the moment a little more emotional was the fact that we would be moving farther away—to Miami—in the next few weeks for my new assignment. As I held on to her, I reminded her to never forget who she is and what she believed—and that I was confident she was going to be amazing.

Jess would call home quite regularly to catch us up on her new journey in college. During one of the calls, it was apparent that Jess was a little frustrated. She began to tell Shelly how many of her friends and acquaintances had parents who were paying for their college and giving monthly stipends.

Shelly reminded Jess about our previous conversations about college: Mom and Dad were not going into debt in order for our children to go to college. Shelly reminded her of our expectation to find a job, get involved on the campus in order to become a resident assistant, and work on decreasing her tuition fees. I had often told Jess—as well as the rest of the kids—that when she graduated college, she would be very proud to look at her degree and realize that she, not Mom and Dad, had worked hard to obtain that piece of paper on the wall. Jessica did just that. By the time she started her sophomore year, she had become a resident assistant, which decreased her tuition a great deal. She also got a job at a local establishment, found a job in the financial aid office, and applied for and received a Connecticut driver's license. She fought for in-state tuition, which she was granted by the college administration.

A few years into her college career, Jess told me that she didn't know if she didn't like her major (meteorology) because it was hard or because she just didn't like it. After speaking for a little while, she let me know that she was changing her major to justice and law. She believed it was a more exciting and suitable major to pursue. I told her that I thought it was a great idea and that she would love the subject matter. Jess would have an extra semester in order to earn her college degree. Following her graduation, she was immediately hired by one of the largest retail stores as a team leader in the security department.

On an early Saturday morning, Shelly walked up to me in the kitchen and said there was something very wrong with Jessica. She went on to say that Jessica told her over the phone that she wanted to quit her job and come back home. Jessica had been out of the house for six years. In that time, Doug had received an appointment to the United States Naval Academy, Mark had received an appointment to the United States Coast Guard Academy, and we had been reassigned to Dallas.

I called Jessica, and she was very emotional. She hated her job and was going to quit. She kept saying, "Daddy, I need to get away from here!" We talked for some time, and it it finally dawned on me that Jessica was in quicksand. She was looking for a lifeline! I told her to go to her supervisor and see if they would transfer her to a store in north Texas. Within the next few weeks, Jess received a transfer and, with some minimal belongings in tow, she drove to our home in north Texas.

The next few weeks were quite an adjustment for the entire family. When Jessica arrived, she was a physical, emotional, and spiritual wreck. At night, we would often hear her crying and sobbing. There were days when she would get into screaming matches with Marissa. It was sobering for Shelly and me to witness our child dealing with so much emotional pain. There were times we secretly wondered if the confident and bold child we knew would move beyond the pain and regrets and pursue her purpose in life.

Several weeks later, I heard her sobbing in her room late one night—and decided I had to speak with her. As I walked into her room, I could see she was physically distraught. Shelly and I had noticed that she seemed to be void of any joy since she arrived. As we began to talk, she confided in me about regrets, failures, and the shame of wasted time in an unproductive and toxic relationship. She was literally grieving about the path she had walked.

In the midst of our discussion, I said, "Jess, when you were involved in that relationship, walking on that path, you knew it was the wrong path and the wrong direction, didn't you?"

"Yes," she said. "I knew all along, but I did it anyway and wasted so much time!"

"No, Jess. It was not a waste of time. It was a lesson you had to learn in order to grow. You should look back and recognize what you learned from that walk and realize that God never, ever abandons His children—even when we walk away." I had the opportunity to tell Jess about my own struggles and failures as a young man before I met her mom. I told her that I shackled myself to my past failures until I learned that I could never reach my God-given future if I continued to live in the past. I told her what our pastor would often remind us: the failures of our past are not the headlines for our future![34] Finally, I told her to that she needed to be willing to accept and learn from her past and start walking toward her God-appointed destiny.

A few weeks later, I sat with Jessica again to let her know our expectations for her in the coming year. "Mom and I have talked, and you have one year to get your stuff together. You have one year—and no more—to find a place to live. You have one year to find out what you should pursue in terms of a career if you hate your current job. I was about to go on when she interrupted and stated, "Daddy, all I ever wanted to be … all I ever wanted to really become … is a police officer!"

I was initially a little taken aback, but after some discussion and thought, I realized I should have seen it coming. When she was a little girl, she always wanted to wear my DEA raid jacket. She would wear cowboy boots with her brother's toy guns in her pants while pushing a baby carriage, saying how she was going to get the "bad guys." I told her if she believed that God was calling her toward that profession— then she should pursue it with all her heart.

We watched with a great sense of relief and pride as Jess began to change overnight in pursuit of her calling. Although she would face a few speed bumps in her new walk, she started to heal emotionally. Her joy returned as she started to once again attend church regularly. She also began a rigorous workout routine since she would be required to pass a physical conditioning test, which included an obstacle course as a requirement for acceptance to the police academy.

As each day passed, she became more confident in her pursuit. Her entire physical demeanor was changing for the better. Her only main challenge in preparation for passing the physical standards was attempting to scale a six-foot wall. She would get so frustrated because she believed scaling the wall was more mental than physical—and she was right. Throughout her application process, I never attempted to assist her. I told her that she never wanted anyone to say how her daddy helped her get on the police department. It was about her ability to focus and pursue her goals, and it would take sacrifice and perseverance on her part.

I knew I had to do something to build her confidence for scaling the wall—so I built one in the backyard. When she came home from work, I told her there would be no excuse not to get over the wall since she could practice daily for the test. In fact, she would practice morning and night to scale the wall and passed the physical standards test with ease.

We watched her evolve into a woman who was driven by purpose and passion. In less than a year, Jessica would move out on her own, receive an appointment to a major police department's academy, and begin her new calling as a public servant. Since that time, she has grown in her Christian walk, excelled in her profession, met and married a wonderful man of faith and purpose—and has recently given birth to her son Brayden David.

Watching our children go through seasons of pain, adversity, and sometimes failure is extremely difficult. Our natural and almost instinctual reaction is to immediately shield them or remove them from the situation and/or alleviate the temporary struggle they are grappling with. We often want to take their pain or failure as our burden. The reality is that, although it is painful to watch, there is purpose in the pain our children endure.

In his senior year of high school, Mark received a full scholarship through an ROTC program in a small college in the Northwest. While he was genuinely excited about the scholarship opportunity, Mark, like his older brother, wanted to pursue an appointment to a military academy. Although his test scores and GPA were not high enough to receive a direct appointment, he was afforded an opportunity to attend the US Coast Guard Academy Prep School for a year before receiving an appointment to the US Coast Guard Academy. From a very young age, Mark was very dedicated and committed to pursuing his calling of one day leading men and women in public service.

Throughout his time at prep school and the academy, Mark pushed and clawed his way through the academic rigors. Every day was an academic struggle for him, and the fear of getting thrown out of the academy for academic failure was something he lived with constantly.

He told Shelly that he thought about three things every day: "I think about girls, God, and getting thrown out of here!" We would have dozens and dozens of conversations about never giving up. I would say, "You make them throw you out before you ever quit!"

At the end of his junior year, after receiving his class ring and his ceremonial saber, he called to let me know he was being assigned to a patrol boat in Santa Barbara for his summer assignment. He said, "Pop, I am almost there—just one more year!"

Just a week into his summer assignment, Mark was ordered back to the academy on the recommendation from an academic review board that decided he would be dismissed for failing an advanced physics course. He was given an opportunity to appeal the decision, and Mark wrote an appeal to the commandant.

I have been told by some that because of my academic weakness that I don't measure up, that I don't belong here, that I am not officer material, but I refused to believe this and I don't believe it now. I am not at all minimizing the fact that academics have not been my strongest attribute, but for the past three years, I have proven time and time again that walking away or resigning was never an option for me. I truly believe that I am called to serve as a warrior no matter how hard or how long it takes ... I recognize the precarious situation I am in and I am troubled and afraid, but giving up is just not in my nature. I cannot and will not promise that if given the opportunity that I will suddenly become an A student. What I can promise is that Mark Capra will never give up. I will endeavor to endure, to drive forward.[35]

After almost three months of waiting, Mark received the news that his appeal was denied. When he called me to let me know, I could hear the absolute disappointment and pain. It brought me to my knees as his father. He was severely crushed—emotionally and spiritually. He was escorted back to his dorm to pack out by a senior non-commissioned officer who did his best to encourage Mark to pursue his dream. Pushing through the emotional pain of rejection and failure, Mark said, "I was raised a champion, and I will get back up!" Prior to leaving the academy grounds, Mark met with the commandant of cadets who wrote him a note and encouraged him to finish college and pursue a commission through the Coast Guard's Officer Candidate School (OCS).

Though dealing with the emotional pain and rejection of being dismissed for academic weakness, Mark pursued his passion to be a public servant. He sought, applied, and was granted a transfer to the University of North Texas in order to complete his bachelor's degree. He decided to apply to OCS after graduation, and if that didn't work out, he was determined to become a police officer. He graduated with above average grades and received an interview with the OCS panel at the same time he applied for and started the process to be hired as a police officer in an adjacent city to where Jessica was serving.

Following his interview with a coast guard panel, he was advised that he did extremely well and that the admission board would meet within the next few months. A week before the OCS board met, Mark was contacted and asked to provide his prep school transcripts.

Something didn't sound right to me, and I asked him why they would need his prep scores since they were not transferable to other academic institutions.

Mark didn't know why and had his prep school transcripts overnighted to the board. Two days later Mark was notified that he was not accepted to OCS because his prep school GPA brought his overall GPA lower than a 2.5, disqualifying him from entrance into OCS.

I was absolutely enraged. I was convinced that someone was bound and determined to keep him from becoming a coast guard officer because of his dismissal from the academy. I thought, *Really, God? You want to put this kid through the emotional ringer again?*

When I calmed down I sat with Mark and said, "Son, sometimes things happen in your life that are unfair. In fact, they are simply unjust. Apparently God has closed that door for you, and you have to decide how you will respond and what your next step will be."

Mark didn't miss a beat. He was not going to let that news get in the way of moving forward. He declared that he was going to pursue a calling in public service and finish the application process for the police department.

His drive, determination, and passion in pursuit of his calling led him to being appointed as the police academy class president. He was subsequently selected as the class spokesman during graduation. During his speech, Shelly and I were brought to tears as he began to speak.

> My name is Mark Capra, and I have the privilege of being class president. Growing up, my father always taught me that we are preparing for the next season.

Always in training for what's to come. "Sacrifice now for the prize in the end," he would say, "and train like you fight and when the fight comes, you will fight like you train."

We have been training for the next season; however, it has been my experience that no matter how hard you train, it is nothing like what is really going to happen. It's nothing like the real thing. So, the truth is we don't know. We don't know what to expect even with all this training and preparing. We are headed into the unknown.

Here is what the last six months have taught me and my classmates about the unknown, what all these long hours at the gym and at training locations prepared us for. It prepared us to be physically, emotionally, and spiritually ready to face the unknown

Physically, we have to be ready to fight. To enter the arena when bell rings and know that even before the fight's on, you've already won. Your muscles have been torn time and time again. Any foe who dares to challenge you has no right to be in the same arena.

Emotionally, it prepared us for the emotional roller coaster that we will experience day to day and the stress it will have on us. And finally, spiritually, to be of sound body and mind to make the life and death decisions that we will only have seconds to decide.

You must all understand that this profession is honorable. There are only a chosen few with the warrior spirit. To run toward danger while the others run away. It is a calling to be a guardian.

Plato says this, "In a republic that honors the core ideals of democracy; the greatest amount of power is given to those called the guardians. Only those with most impeccable character are given the responsibility of protecting the democracy."

Even before the academy, you were being called to be something greater. You lived a life of challenges and struggle. This life of struggle wasn't in vain; it was a test. It was testing you for impeccable character. And it led you here ... to the training grounds of the guardians of democracy.[36]

By the end of his speech, Shelly and I were in tears—and were witness to the rousing applause and cheers from his classmates and the audience who witnessed his heartfelt message to his crew. There are times as parents when we prayed that the time, training, and discipline in raising children would benefit to our kids. It was clear to me that Mark was more prepared to face the unknown than I was at his age.

As we looked back at Mark and Jessica's journey, Shelly and I were reminded that we can see the unmistakable pattern designed by a loving God who reminds us that—even in our trials, weakness, failures, and shortcomings—He never abandons his children who are called by His name. Mark's incredible journey, though at times painful, actually led him to meeting with his beautiful and talented wife who is an outstanding woman of purpose and faith.

There is purpose in our children's pain, purpose in their adversity, and purpose in their failures although it is often difficult to fully comprehend while we witness their walk during these seasons. Through it all, Shelly and I learned that we had to allow our children to deal with the trying seasons that are often necessary for growth and maturity, especially in preparation for dealing with a fallen world and a cowardly culture.

CHAPTER 12

PREPARING FOR MARRIAGE

When Shelly and I were first engaged, I constantly asked God not to let me screw things up. Part of the reason was because of some of my insecurities and failures in my past, and the other part was that I knew the man looking back at me in the mirror—his dark side, fears, and shortcomings.

Prior to meeting Shelly, I would often ask God if He really had someone for me to love and be loved by. I wanted very much to be the kind of man who my future wife would be proud of. Shelly was the absolute answer to that prayer. She has always been my biggest advocate and strongest supporter. She has encouraged me to pursue my calling and my dreams since our earliest days of dating. We are very much alike in a number of ways, but she is smarter, has better relational and leadership skills, and is able to juggle a number of priorities at once. I have jokingly told a number of audiences that if men want to have a successful marriage and life, marry way up like I did!!

Divorce was never in our lexicon throughout any season in our marriage. Shelly and I were fortunate to have parents who were great role models. Regardless of their advice, we learned that marriage was not always easy—and it took work and commitment from both of us. Several months before getting married, my mom told us that— no matter what other people said—marriage is not a give-and-take situation. True marriage is a give-and-give relationship because when one person gives, the other receives. It was and is a profound pearl of wisdom that took a little time to sink in for me.

After Jessica was back with us in north Texas for about a month, we went out for breakfast. During some small talk over eggs and coffee, she said, "You know, Dad, you and Mom are a fairy tale to most people."

I was puzzled by her statement and asked what she meant. Her expression turned somber and she said, "Dad, I don't have a single friend who has the same mom and dad who have been together. In fact, most of my friends' parents have been remarried more than twice or are currently divorced and single!"

I didn't know how to respond, but after a few moments, I said, "Mom and I are far from a fairy tale. We are more like a dark comedy. The reality of it is that we have worked hard and promised each other we would never quit until it killed us. You see, Jess, you never see behind the curtain—the pain and struggle it took to make sure we did our best, not only with each other but in raising you kids. You never saw the arguments, the fighting about expenses, and the private struggles we both dealt with spiritually and emotionally. But you know what, Jess? Every painful struggle had a purpose; most of that time, it was for our growth as a husband and wife and as parents. I wouldn't change a single day, but I am sure Mom may have wanted to."

She laughed, and I went on to discuss a little more about what we learned throughout our marriage.

When you choose to enter into marriage, you must be willing to be committed to the growth and development of your spouse. You must be willing to put aside your wants and selfish desires in order to meet the needs of your wife or husband, and that takes time to learn. Again, this is not a give-and-take exchange. It is a give-and-give exchange that builds a covenant relationship. Unfortunately, in our culture, we no longer pursue covenant relationships or teach the importance of what that means. I have often said that many couples enter a marriage relationship with a twisted sense of their vows in the back of their mind, such as: *I take you in sickness and in health or until something better comes along!*

The term covenant means "a coming together." It is a commitment that binds two parties together and carries with it the concept of cleaving to one another as if to bind our self to that other person for a great purpose.[37] Covenants are the fruit of a faithful relationship of trust; therefore, covenant partners take responsibility for their actions and nurture their relationship.

The reality is that we live in a "throwaway" culture that celebrates selfishness and no longer values working hard in order to build relationships of trust. In the past several decades, the evidence would suggest that many young married couples no longer expect a relationship of trust; within the first few years of marriage, many begin to expect deception and/or infidelity both real and imagined. That is why some people decide to initiate prenuptial agreements, which are nothing more than contracts to protect individual interests in the case of a divorce. Most contracts are based on protection, mistrust, and deceit. Just imagine, for a moment, the cost of the emotional, physical, and mental stress and pain when a marital relationship is based upon the notion that one party will ultimately be deceived.

If the numbers are correct—and there is great disagreement by researchers—one in two marriages ends in divorce in our country compared to just over twenty-five years ago. While we recognize there may be a host of reasons that lead to divorce, Shelly and I have witnessed firsthand that many couples enter into marriage with a number of misperceptions and/or never really consider the enormity and sacredness of a marriage covenant. We spent a great deal of time talking to the kids about how that marriage is a sacred commitment not to be entered into lightly.

On occasion, we discussed with the kids how people could be enamored and excited about meeting, dating, and marrying someone who is the complete opposite of them. The reality is that the excitement only lasts a short time. You finally wake up one day and realize that you have nothing in common with the person next to you. That begins the struggle of how not being equally yoked impacts the marital relationship. A yoke is a wooden bar that joins two oxen to each other and to the burden they pull. An "unequally yoked" team has one stronger ox and one weaker, or one taller and one shorter. The weaker or shorter ox would walk more slowly than the taller, stronger one, causing the load to go around in circles. When oxen are unequally yoked, they cannot perform the task set before them. Instead of working together, they are actually fighting against each other.[38]

It is important to understand that we believe that being equally yoked has nothing to do with a couples' similar looks, education, financial status, or physical appearance. More importantly, being equally yoked has everything to do with whether you and your future husband or wife is of the same faith and believers in the Word of God. Being equally yoked is no guarantee that you will have a successful and blessed marriage, especially if one chooses to ignore his or her covenant responsibilities. Our definition of being unequally yoked does not mean a marriage will ultimately fail, but it does present some challenges, especially when children come along. Once again, the divorce rates throughout the Christian community are about the same as the secular world.

Douglas was the first of our children to be married. When we first met Kirsten, Doug's wife, who I have always called "Cookie," Doug was finishing his senior year at the US Naval Academy. When it became apparent that they were getting serious, Shelly and I met with them privately. Although they were both grounded in their faith, we wanted to discuss the realities of married life, especially for those who marry into a life of public service. Doug would soon graduate and be commissioned as a United States Marine Corps officer. Following the completion of his training, he would be sent to theater operations in Afghanistan. Our talk with them was not about us questioning whether they really wanted to get married; it was about what they should expect from each other and what they could absolutely expect from a corrupt culture when they married.

I began by telling them that after they finished chasing each other around the house naked for the first few weeks, they would wake up one morning and realize that they are bound to each other for the rest of their lives. I reminded them both that marriage is not a tryout. It is to be pursued as a sacred commitment between a husband and wife. The most important piece of advice we could give them was to encourage them to pray with each other constantly and to ask the Lord to bless them and their marriage. We urged them to establish a habit of praying with each other daily if possible. I said, "Doug, I pray that when you reached my age, you will look at Cookie the way I look at Mom every day. You see your mother as your mom, as you should, through the eyes of a son, her child. Doug, when I look at your mom, I see the wife of my youth, who still stirs my heart with her love and intimacy, and I hope and pray you see the same thing in your wife when you have children of your own."

We discussed a number of other things, including how they would run into other men and women who would actually try to pursue them romantically because they saw them as a challenge, a mark of accomplishment if they could get them to fail each other. Shelly and I explained how marriage would not protect them from the trappings of a fallen culture. If anything, the snares become harder to see because they are sometimes clouded in seductive compliments and the suggestions of others who are intent on watching you fall. We reminded them to never talk negatively about each other to anyone since it dishonors the spouse. We advised them to give themselves to each other freely and learn to forgive each other quickly.

We told them that they must continue to fight for each other in the arena, which will take work, sacrifice, and establishing habits that are developed out of their love and commitment for each other. It is worth it, especially when you learn to fully lean on and trust God in pursuing your marital relationship.

Following our talk, Shelly and I blessed them as parents in asking God's favor and protection on them, their marriage, and their lives together. Four of our six children are now married, and Shelly and I had a similar conversation with each of them.

When Jess went off to the police academy, I warned her about what I called "academy love." When you live and work in close quarters every day in a profession that requires you to totally trust and rely on your partners, you can develop an unrealistic sense of who that guy or gal really is. My caution to her was disregarded as we soon met Jim

Brad Ortiz, a young faithful man who was a classmate at the police academy. Brad would soon pursue Jess with all of his might. I could see in his eyes and in his demeanor that he worshipped the ground my daughter walked on. In just a few years, he would ask me permission to marry her. I have always described Brad like one of my sons. He is large and loud, and Shelly and I love him and are thankful that the good Lord provided such a man of purpose and faith for my daughter. As of this writing, they have entered a new season since the arrival of their firstborn son.

I was definitely more critical when my girls were contemplating marriage. As a father, the first thing I would think about was if the man was going to be able to protect my little girl. Would he really be a warrior for her and for her children? Fathers often have a certain type of man in mind to marry daughters, but it is rarely the case.

For my last two years with the DEA, I was working in Washington and commuting home every four to six weeks. As I prepared to fly home one Thursday, shortly before Christmas, Rebecca called to ask if she could bring her friend Jason over the house on Friday—and stay for the night. Becky was attending college in Oklahoma, and I had heard that she had been seeing this young man for a little while. I would find out that Jason was also attending college in Oklahoma. Like Becky, he was a musical theater major. Because I can be a class-A chucklehead at times, I thought, A musical theater major? This should be interesting!

When I arrived at the house with refreshments and groceries for the weekend, Shelly—being her typical warm and bubbly wife and mom—greeted me and then introduced me to Becky's friend. Jason Bias was wearing a blue cardigan, khaki pants, and a pair of loafers. He was holding a glass of red wine by the stem, and suddenly the chuckleheaded, knuckle-dragging caveman in me started to come out.

As Jason shook my hand and greeted me warmly, I think I may have grunted hello. Throughout the rest of the night, shamefully, I did my best not to talk much to him—even though Shelly kept pushing me to spend time with him. I did do a lot of listening as Jason and Becky talked to all the other kids about the different musicals they were in, the songs they sang, and the Broadway shows they intended to go to.

By the end of the night, I was determined that there was no way that my daughter should be dating this guy.

After Jason left the house the next morning, I spoke with Becky out under the porch. With absolutely no regard for my daughter's feelings—and without asking her anything about her relationship with Jason—I began to tell her that there was no way she should be dating him. During my one-way conversation, I said, "This is not the man for you!"

Becky has a beautiful, pleasing, and caring spirit, and she just sat there nodding with tears streaming down her face.

I said, "God knows the plans for you Becky—plans for good!" When I was finished, I gave her a hug and went inside. I thought, As it is written, so it shall be done!

We made it through the rest of the holiday season with no further discussion and without seeing any more of Jason.

A few weeks into the New Year, Shelly called me at work to tell me about a conversation she just had with Becky. Becky actually broke up with Jason after my talk, but they were dating again. Becky said, "He makes me happy, he loves the Lord, and we are so much alike. I like him a lot, Mom, and we are going to see each other!" Shelly told me how proud she was of Becky for standing her ground and making her own decision about their relationship.

Following our conversation, I started to consider that I might have been off a little regarding Jason. Five minutes later, my phone rang again.

Becky said, "Daddy, did Mom tell you about the relationship?"

I couldn't help but say, "What relationship?"

Becky went on to say that this young man made her happy and that she liked being with him.

I paused for a moment and then said, "If he makes you happy and continues to respect and honor you, Becky, that is a good thing."

We talked a little more, and I heard in her voice how desperately she wanted me to like Jason.

It took me some time to realize how much I mishandled everything about the situation. The more I got to know Jason, the more I grew to love and respect him. I witnessed how he loved and cherished my daughter. I soon became acutely aware of my initial arrogance and pride as a father—as well as my lack of faith that God would bless my daughter's pursuit of a husband.

It took me about a year to realize what a hypocrite I was since I was the guy running around and telling my kids and others how not to judge others by their looks or views or opinions. I always told them that they should take time to love people and remember to trust and have faith that God is able to work out all things. In one brief meeting, I made such a poor judgment of a young man that I completely disregarded my faith and wisdom and attempted to insert myself as God by decreeing that I knew what was best for my daughter. How absolutely arrogant, foolish, and prideful I was. I had to wrestle with my shameful conduct and hoped that my daughter and her future husband would forgive me someday.

I had been retired for just a few months when Jason contacted me and asked to meet him at a local cigar bar. I had come to know Jason quite well and knew that, since he didn't smoke and rarely consumed any type of alcohol, he was preparing to ask me permission to marry Rebecca. When we met at the establishment, I could see that Jason was extremely nervous, fidgeting with his hands while making general conversation about Becky.

During our initial conversation, I said, "Jason, I need to apologize to you for how I acted when I first met you. For whatever stupid reason, I initially believed that you were not right for my daughter. I realized that I was very wrong and who was I to get in the way of what God would ordain?"

Jason was kind and gracious and finally got around to asking for permission to marry Becky.

During their beautiful wedding ceremony, our pastor, Toby Slough told the congregation how he had prayed that God would give him a special word or scripture specifically for Becky and Jason. Toby looked at them and told them that the Lord had impressed on his heart this scripture: "For I know the plans I have for you, plans for good and not for evil, to give you a future and a hope."

Our entire family literally gasped and began to weep. It was Jeremiah 29:11—the same scripture the kids had grown up with, the same scripture I had previously repeated so arrogantly to Becky years earlier. Now, in this moment, we were sure that Lord was simply confirming to us all as a family that He is and always was a lamp to our feet. I told Shelly it was if the Lord sort of winked at us in that moment as if to say, "Hey, guys. I got this. In fact, I always did!"

About six months after Becky and Jason's wedding, Mark and Christine got married. Mark's journey through adversity and trials ultimately led him to dating, falling in love, and marrying Christine, who was nursing student at Baylor University. Shelly and I were once again amazed and thankful to witness what we believed to be a divine pattern of how they both came to meet and fall in love.

When Mark proposed to Christine, we held a wonderful engagement celebration with both families and friends at our home. Toward the end of the night, Marissa placed her head on my shoulder and asked, "Daddy, is there somebody out there for me?"

I laughed and reminded her that I had always told her that somewhere there is a man who is in training to be her husband. I jokingly told her that God is taking His time molding that man because she was such a great catch.

She had a sad expression and said, "Dad, I am getting so old—and I don't even have a boyfriend yet!"

I laughed because Rissy had just turned twenty-one and was in the process of finishing her undergraduate degree at a local university.

She was very serious about her question. So for the second time, I had the opportunity to tell one of my daughters about my own walk and concerns in wondering if God had a wife for me. It might have been the champagne or the climate of the celebration, but as I walked her through my journey of meeting Shelly, I began to get emotional. I told her how, after I began to fall in love with her mom, I begged God to not let me mess up. I was so insecure and scared that I wasn't good enough for her. While desperately trying to hold back my tears, I told her how blessed I was that her mom said yes and that we were still going strong thirty-four years later.

"Your mother has always, always made me better at everything I do. You know what, Rissy? I love just being in the same room as Mom!"

With tears running down her face, Rissy hugged me and yelled, "Shelly, you better appreciate the husband you have!"

Shelly told her she did while looking at me quizzically and trying to figure out what just occurred.

We have tried to do our best in teaching and training our children up in what it takes to prepare for marriage. We did our best to explain how important it was to be equally yoked and to develop a covenant relationship, and we recognized that it was important for them to witness how Shelly and I treated and acted toward each other. While they would witness how we argued on occasion, we were never afraid to show our open affection toward each other. The kids would often catch us stealing a kiss or a hug. When they were much younger, they would simply giggle when they saw us kiss. When they were older, especially as teens, they would pretend to gag and say, "Get a room!"

While I was preparing to retire from the DEA, I sent a message to all of my children to let them know why I made my decision.

> Kids, I wanted to take a moment to share with you some things as I prepare to retire. It is important to me, especially given the significance of the timing as today is Father's Day. I want you to understand that the primary reason for my retirement is really simple: I love your mother so very much and can no longer stand to be away from her for long periods of time. The love of my job, my position in my agency, or the status as a government executive can never compare to the absolute joy and contentment I have just being in the same room, the same house, the same area with the woman God has sought fit to bless me with. I pray that when you all reach our age, you feel the same way about the man or woman God has for you.
>
> When I look back on my career, I marvel at how God continues to bless me, to bless us as a family, and

I am thankful, thankful for the children He saw fit to bless me with as well. I always, always strived to raise you the way a good and godly father should, but I know at times I made many mistakes. Because of my calling, you were constantly uprooted from state to state and left new and old friends behind. Yet no matter where we landed, you all thrived and excelled. And now as I look at you all, I see how you all have grown into men and women of great character, men and women who love the Lord, men and women with purpose and commitment who choose to walk the path He has designed for you. No father could be as proud as I am of all of you, and I love, just absolutely love being your dad! Pops [39]

We are extremely thankful to have been blessed to be the parents of six outstanding children of faith, purpose, and passion. We have struggled to raise them to be courageous men and women of faith who willingly pursue truth and integrity in their daily walks and throughout the remainder of their respective lives. We have watched with great pride and with a heart of thanksgiving as each of our children left our covering and pursued a path designed by a loving and faithful God. We recognize as parents that their journeys, struggles, and challenges are just beginning, but we are confident that we have more than prepared them to live, learn, and thrive in a cowardly culture and a fallen world.

It is our hope and desire that our walk and experience will give others hope and strength to take up their God-given role as parents, regardless of circumstances. There are no perfect parents just as there are no perfect children. You simply have to be willing to enter the arena and be prepared to fight for their hearts and minds.

The arena calls us all, but you must understand that you will pay a price because getting into the arena is work. Getting into the arena takes time. Getting into the arena takes sacrifice and risk. At times, the battle seems hopeless. In the arena, our faith is tested and sharpened as fire does to steel. It is in the arena where courage and determined perseverance births hope. It is in the arena where love and forgiveness will be found; and it is in the arena where "the prayers of a righteous man availeth much."[40]

Our journey as parents is far from over, and even now, we continue to grow and learn as we prepare for the next generation of our children's children. We hope and pray that this book about our journey has encouraged you as you continue to walk your path as a parent determined to raise your own warrior to face an unpredictable and cowardly culture.

AFTERWORD

Shelly and I are both excited and sometimes a little concerned as we prepare to enter the next season of our lives. From our vantage point, we continue to witness the ongoing assault on truth amidst a cultural revolution, the continual denigration of marriage, the destruction of the American family, and the outright hatred and mockery of Judeo-Christian ethics, morals, and faith.

It would be easy to simply give up, lock our doors, and become the angry old people at the end of the cul-de-sac, but that's just not who we are. We realized very early in our marriage that our culture was steadily heading in a downward spiral, which motivated us to do our best in raising children who are courageous and willing to fight back against a culture that would do everything to force them to conform. It was never our goal to raise six clones. We wanted to raise faithful men and women who would respond to a failing culture with love, respect, and dignity in pursuit of the truth. We remain quite proud and delight in watching as they pursue their callings in life.

Jessica and Brad have been married for a little more than three years. They both work as police officers for a large city in north Texas and have both received a number of commendations and accolades for their performance as public servants. They are enjoying their new roles as a mom and dad to their first born baby boy, Brayden David.

Douglas and Cookie have been married for more than five years and live in North Carolina. Doug is a US Marine Corps officer and has completed three combat tours in Afghanistan. Cookie is currently working for one of the largest government contractors in the United

States. They are currently preparing for their next season as they decide whether to remain on active duty or move into the private and/or public service sector.

Mark and Christine have been married for four months and live in north Texas. Mark is a police officer in a sister city of where Jess and Brad work, and Christine is a registered nurse at a pediatric oncology hospital.

Becky and Jason have been married for just over a year. Becky works as a training instructor for a national mammography center, and Jason works as the creative arts director for one of the largest churches in north Texas. They continue to pursue acting and performing in a number of plays and musicals in the area. I keep telling them that I will be their security director when they make it big—but it will cost them!

Marissa, my strong-willed child, is finishing her last year in college in north Texas, majoring in communications. Marissa is a very gifted speaker and is wise beyond her years. A friend recently told me how Marissa was on a church panel with women twice her age, and they were all amazed by her wisdom and knowledge about the subject at hand. She also has an incredible gift of discernment and has a heart for the mission field. Marissa gave up her junior and senior spring breaks during high school in order to serve in Mumbai, India, with her church family. Shelly and I are very excited to see where and how the good Lord is going to use her. We have no doubt that she will be amazingly awesome no matter what she pursues!

Our youngest child, Micah—who we lovingly call Shrek—received an appointment to the US Air Force Academy and is currently in his sophomore year. Micah, who we almost lost when he was a baby, towers over the rest of his brothers and sisters. Doug and Mark are convinced that the breathing treatments he had to perform when he was young had some type of steroids in them, and that's why he is so big. Micah has his own unique story in that he really wanted to play football for the US Naval Academy, but he was not afforded the opportunity. He decided to commit to a small Christian college outside of Saint Louis to play football and pursue an ROTC program. Just a few days after his committal, he was summoned to his athletic director's office where he was approached by a coach from the US Air Force Academy. Apparently, the coach reviewed footage of Micah's athletic ability playing varsity football and asked him to consider playing for the Air Force Falcons. He subsequently signed with Air Force and received an appointment to the academy after successfully completing a year at the Air Force Prep School.

Shelly and I continue to love our home here in north Texas, and we have no plans to move again. We have continually been asked if we plan on downsizing, but we just respond that we are waiting for all the grandchildren we hope to have here someday. Shelly is currently pursuing a new opportunity working in IT within the health care industry and I continue to write and speak around the country on contemporary leadership issues, national security, and family and parenting challenges.

One of our biggest concerns in writing this book has been that some would view it as a how-to book or think we somehow hold all the answers to parenting. It is not, and we don't—and that really should be very clear. If we had to share only a couple of things as one parent to the next, we would simply say to never give up and to constantly seek the wisdom of a loving God who loves you and your children regardless of your current situation.

Throughout this book, we have consistently referred to our faith in a loving, caring, merciful, and personal God who knows us by name. It is not a popular position today to be a flawed person of strong Christian faith, but that is who we are. For those readers who are unfamiliar with what we are speaking about in terms of our faith, I would like to share further.

We believe that all of creation cries out that God exists and that He is a personal Lord who yearns to have a relationship with His creation. We believe that the Bible is the inspired Word of God and that it is a love story about God's creation, human frailty, sin, failure, and His redemption for a fallen world through Jesus Christ.

John 3:16 says "For God so loved the world that He gave His only begotten Son for whosoever believes in Him, will not perish but have everlasting life."[41] It doesn't say that you have to be perfect. It doesn't say that you have to have so many good deeds. It doesn't say that you have to become something you are not. It's a promise for anyone who believes. When Jesus was crucified on the cross, He was crucified along with two thieves. One mocked Jesus while the other said that they deserved their punishment and asked Jesus to remember him. In the midst of His tremendous suffering, bloodshed, and pain, Jesus said, "Today you will be with me in paradise."[42] The thief wasn't required to pray a special prayer, give money, or be a certain denomination. He just asked Jesus for mercy and forgiveness in his own way, and Jesus said yes—with no strings attached and no hidden requirements!

We realize that the concept of a personal, un-caused creator of the universe is foreign and akin to a fairy tale for many in our culture, and it is often met with mockery and disbelief. Some of that is due to false and flawed teachings that have been spewed, but much has to do with the human heart. Our sin nature simply refuses to believe that we are created in the image of a loving and just Creator who desires a relationship with us (His creation).

We don't believe that that we are somehow part of the happy, holy, healthy, wealthy club because we are Christians. Jesus even warned that we would be hated because of Him. For those of you who are not sure or who are on the fence about this God thing, we simply recommend asking Him to show you if He is what we say He is. Be prepared to see how He responds.

We only have a moment here—and only so many breaths. What will your legacy be when you die? What will be on your tombstone? If you are fortunate to be in your bed and conscious as you are preparing to take your last breath, who will be at your bedside?

None of us on our deathbed will wish we had one more day to make a buck, one more sale, or one more minute at the office. We will all regret that we should have loved more, forgiven more, or spent more time with family.

Shelly and I realize that we only have a minute here. Our time is brief, and we recognize that we have more years behind us than ahead of us. We are comfortable with our mortality because we know our eternal destination. We still long to finish well and continue to make a difference in the lives of our family as well as others we come into contact with.

Regardless of a failing and cowardly culture—regardless of those who mock our faith, values, and beliefs—we will continue to speak boldly with confidence, love, and respect about the importance of training and preparing the next generation to face the challenges and battles that await them.

Jim and Shelly Capra on wedding day
(photo by "Jerry")

Jim and Shelly Capra circa 2015
(Photo by Donna Sweetin)

Our six crew members circa 1999
(Photo by Shelly Capra)

Our crew at Jim's Retirement 2014
Left to Right Micah, Marissa, Rebecca, Mark, Douglas, Jessica
(Photo by Michelle Capra)

Shelly's Dad and Mom
Cyril and Emily Polacheck circa 2000
(Photo by Shelly Capra)

Jim's Mom, "G" surrounded by our crew circa 2011
(Photo by Michelle Capra)

Officer Jessica Ortiz
(Photo by Shelly Capra)

Captain Douglas Capra, USMC
(Photo by Stars and Stripes circa 2014)

Left to Right: Jessica, Mark, Jim
(Photo by Michelle Capra)

Our Blue Line here in North Texas
Left to Right: Brad, Mark, Jessica
(Photo by Michelle Capra)

Rebecca starring in a Musical "Sing For Your Supper" circa 2012
(Photo by Wendy Mutz)

Jason Proposing to Rebecca on stage in front of the cast of
"Once" at the Dallas Windspear Opera House Circa 2014
(Photo by Angela Platt)

Marissa comforting her Dad during his retirement circa 2014
(photo by Michelle Capra)

Micah on the AFA Football Field
(photo by Donna Sweetin)

Our Courageous Crew!!

Left to Right: Brad Ortiz, Jason Bias, Mark Capra, Micah
Capra, Doug Capra, Cookie Capra, Christine Capra,
Marissa Capra, Rebecca Bias, Jessica Ortiz.
(photo by Michelle Capra)